The
Right to Hunt

by

James B. Whisker

Foreword

by

Bud Shuster

N

North River Press

Library of Congress Cataloging in Publication Data

Whisker, James B., 1939-
    The right to hunt.

    Bibliography: p.
    1. Hunting--History.   2. Hunting--Philosophy.
I. Title.
SK21.W46   175   81-1524
ISBN 0-88427-042-4   AACR2

Manufactured in the United States of America

Contents

For
James B. II and Erik Zane

Foreword

The First Congress of the United States lost little time in seeking to make specific certain of the freedoms implicit in the then new Constitution. The first ten amendments — known as the Bill of Rights — left no doubts about the feelings of those original Members of Congress, or those of the legislators of the several ratifying states.

However, despite this early effort at constitutional precision, questions about the meaning of the Bill of Rights continue to be raised, and frequently in the courts. This is the case with the Second Amendment and its statement concerning "the right of the people to keep and bear arms."

From the first, the key question concerning this amendment has been whether the reason for the right to keep and bear arms was dependent upon the need for "a well regulated militia . . . necessary to the security of a free state."

Today — just as in 1789 — there are those who insist that the need for a "Minuteman" type of militia must determine the people's right "to keep and bear arms." And now, just as then, there are those who insist that this right should not depend on the need for a militia.

Dr. James B. Whisker has written his latest book, *The Right to Hunt,* against the backdrop of this historic argument. His wide-ranging scholarship, his rigorous argument, and his felicity of expression make this an unusual and important work. I commend it to the attention of all of those who, regardless of their position on the continuing argument, share an interest in the Second Amendment and its role in our national life.

Bud Shuster
Member of Congress

Preface

I have previously researched the meaning of the Second Amendment to the Constitution of the United States and discovered, to my satisfaction, that there is a substantial and abiding right to keep and bear arms. In that book, *Our Vanishing Freedom*, I touched lightly on the issue of hunting. In the absence of major literature exploring that issue, I have decided to provide this inquiry.

There is an historic and legal right to hunt. This conclusion is compelled by the overwhelming evidence of man's history as a civilized and rational being. There is little but the rhetoric of an antihunting movement that suggests the contrary.

In researching this book I have been amazed at the antihunting literature. Every major precept of my understanding of religion has been challenged by those who claim that animals have immortal souls and that the beasts of the field have natural or God-given rights. That literature exists in abundance.

The reduction of hunting to a mere fulfillment of an impulse to cruelty or repressed sexual drive is also amazing to me. In these days of amateur neo-Freudian psychology I am not especially surprised, but it does seem to presume that hunters are a sick lot. That again is quite contrary to my own experience.

I admire the successful hunter. I applaud his untiring efforts to stalk the wild animal in its natural habitat and to kill it in its lair. It involves a basic, time-proven conquest of nature. I believe that this is one very basic way man can communicate with nature.

There is a German work of art called the "Hunter's Funeral." The beasts of the forest carry the hunter's coffin on their backs. They respect him for being a great hunter and he them for being worthy objects of the hunt. That painting says much, proving that the single picture is worth a thousand words — or a whole book.

I am indebted to a number of people for their assistance in the preparation of this manuscript. I should note especially a very able student, David Jones, who helped in the legal research and in organizing many materials. Dr. Paul Blackman provided many insights and pointed me in the proper direction on several occasions. I continue to enjoy working with my editor, Bill Cowan. In the final analysis I assume responsibility for all errors of omission and commission.

James B. Whisker
West Virginia University
December 20, 1980

Introduction

Man has been a hunter during his entire existence as a thinking human being. To those who accept the theory of evolution, pre-man was a hunter. Recent research by a team of British physicians suggests that, had man not become a carnivore, his brain would have lacked the necessary fatty acids to have permitted him to function fully. Man could not himself produce these fatty acids from grains, vegetables, nuts, and grasses, and the herbivores that did produce these could not themselves use them to structure their own brains. To those who accept both evolution and a theistic grand design theory, this suggests strongly that, according to that design, man was to eat the flesh of the herbivores as a part of his evolution to mankind.

Man had two probable sources of animal flesh. He could have become either a scavenger or a hunter. Had he not been able to kill his own game, it is doubtful that he could have chased away other predators who did kill. When another animal had made the kill, man might have competed with later scavengers. But man's constitution does not suggest that he could have made a ready diet of scavenged meat on a regular basis. As a tool-making animal, man could probably have hunted and killed his prey by virtue of having a superior technology.

As we observe primitive, even stone-age, man around the world we see that he is a hunter, for the most part, not a scavenger. He utilizes a weapon to kill his prey, and he generally cooks the meat. We also observe that many of the grains, seeds, nuts, and similar vegetable materials require cooking before they can be used. Some are even poisonous to man unless they are cooked first. Since man did not use fire for heating or cooking until late in his evolution, we must conclude that it is highly probable that he hunted before he grew vegetables.

Cultivation of vegetables marks civilized man, or, at least, early man entering that stage just before civilization. Only by settling down in a set area of land could he expect to survive by farming. A vegetarian existence was precarious indeed for a nomad. The evidence suggests that, as relative overpopulation occurred, man was forced to abandon the hunt, for once plentiful game was scarce. Man perhaps did not choose to give up hunting as a way of life; rather, conditions forced him to choose other methods of warding off starvation.

By the time man bcame an agricultural animal he had already developed a ritual surrounding the hunt. Myths of the hunter's prowess at a wide variety of things became attached to his culture. Hunting was thus more than a way of surviving, more than a thing-in-itself. It had many aspects of recreation attached to it long before it was abandoned as the primary way of providing foodstuff to the clan or tribe. In short, hunting became quite early a form of recreation.

As authoritarian governments were formed to control the lives and destinies of men, many prerogatives that had been shared heretofore among all the able-bodied now devolved to the few. No longer could a commoner become the hunter merely by demonstrating that he was a man and should be separated from the women and children. Just as these non-democratic governments created social classes with attendant identification by weapon type, so they divided hunting privileges by class. Nobility and kings could hunt the scarce and elusive large game, mostly, but not entirely, made up of predators, while commoners, if they could hunt at all, were restricted to small game and birds. A new ritual was developed. The kings and their disciples and favorites could prove their manliness by hunting dangerous game, and by clothing themselves in the hides of their kills, while the lower classes had no such opportunity. A military caste of higher level, select troops developed from among the kings' hunters. By royal prerogative they became wholly separated from the non-hunters or the hunters of small game below.

Kings and their courts sectioned off lands to serve as imperial hunting grounds. They practiced a new form of conservation; since only a few could hunt, game species would survive by outnumbering the hunters. Still, like primitive man, no real thought was given by the kings of old to game conservation in the modern sense. Only rarely, as in a reference from the *Book of Mormon,* did early kings try to conserve species. it was a source of secular immortality to be able to say that one had destroyed the last of a species of game, or, at least, that species in a certain area.

Primitive man was probably responsible for destroying several dozen species of game. Historical man probably did not wholly destroy any species of game animal by hunting. But, commonly, he did cause species to become extinct in his known world. Since he did not know that other members of the same species existed elsewhere, the point remains that he did not care to practice conservation and may have received some perverse enjoyment out of his attempt to render a species extinct.

So the Romans nearly destroyed many large species of game in areas of Europe under their control and in North Africa. The later Romans, those who enjoyed the spectacle of the Roman Circus, probably thought they had imported the last of several predator species for their games. But, as was typical of thinking in the late Roman Empire, little thought was given to the events of the next day.

Quietly developing alongside the other empires of the Mediterranean area were the Chosen People of God, the Jews. By the time we meet the Jews of the Old Testament they were already settled into agricuiltural communities. They hunted only rarely, and then for sport. They did kill predators which threatened their herds of sheep or goats. The relative scarcity of game in biblical times precluded regular hunting. We find a few more hunting stories in the apochryphal books than we do in the Bible itself. It is quite possible that the Jewish kings and patriarchs hunted regularly, but there was no real reason to include a recounting of these deeds in the Bible. The Old Testament recognized hunting and attached no onus to it. Indeed, a few hunters, mainly Gentiles, were "mighty hunters." During the Exodus the Jews captured birds by netting them, and that practice apparently continued.

The Jews and Gentiles of the new Testament did not hunt, but they did fish. Christ ate fish and assisted his disciples who earned their living as fishermen. There was no objection to that profession as there was to that of tax collector. Christ distributed the fishes as well as the loaves of bread to his followers. Since most of the disciples were of lower class origin it is probable that they could not hunt; such recreation would have been reserved for the kings, Roman governors, and Roman soldiers.

Continued scarcity of game during the Dark Ages and Middle Ages accounted for hunting being reserved to the kings and their courts. Game laws sought to preserve these privileges for the nobility. The weapons normally associated with the hunt were restricted, partially as a sign of class, and commoners hunted only small game. Certain species were reserved to the nobility, and hunting itself was a sign of noble status.

Clerics enjoyed hunting on the vast church estates. They, too, restricted hunting by commoners. Some medieval clerics sought to support these hunting rights by cautioning the people against the pleasures of hunting as these wordly joys might jeopardize their admission to heaven. John of Salisbury even cautioned kings against enjoying hunting.

Again, overhunting and the lack of meaningful conservation laws and practices made game scarce and even destroyed whole species in some areas. As late as the nineteenth century some nobles delighted at having killed off the last of a game species in an area.

As man came to realize that all men, not just a few, could enjoy natural, perhaps God-given, rights, they sought to enjoy hunting. Coincidentally, the Americas were rediscovered and here there existed a nearly inexhaustible supply of game. Man could again eat meat that he had himself killed in the forests. He need eat vegetables only when he wished. The ready supplies of game saved the early settlers in the Americas.

European man here encountered the native aborigine, the Amerindians. Underpopulation in most of North America had allowed these primitives the luxury of living a nomadic or semi-nomadic hunting life. They killed only what they needed, as there was no incentive to kill more. Still, they did kill in wasteful ways, as in driving herds of bison over cliffs, and by using all-consuming and uncontrolled fires to stampede animals. While they developed a rhetoric that tied man and the animals together in a great web of life under a Great Spirit, they did not hesitate to violate that compact when they discovered they could trade animal hides for trinkets and guns. An explanation of this behavior can be fabricated that exonerates the Amerindian in part. The animal kingdom was blamed for diseases the primitives could not otherwise comprehend. The Amerindian then assumed that the animal kingdom was responsible and made war on it. This may be much more a post-morten fabrication of our imagination than the truth. In any event, the Amerindian did indeed kill off, or nearly killed off, whole species, notably the beaver, in certain areas to satiate his desire for steel knives, guns, beads, blankets, whiskey, and other items that only the whites could supply.

Eventually, whites discovered that they could hunt and trap as well as the Amerindians. Pressures of increasing numbers of Europeans ended in an informal declaration that the Amerindians were obsolete. They must be extinguished or severely controlled if the new lands were to be opened to settlers. Eventually, this was tied to the destruction of the principal food supply of the Amerindians — the bison, or, as commonly known, the buffalo. This convenient confluence of thought and events led the whites to all but render extinct the vast buffalo herds. The Amerindians were controlled only when their mobile and seemingly inexhaustible food supply was destroyed.

But, more generally, the vast game supplies were diminished by the expropriation of their traditional breeding, nesting, and living areas by farmers, ranchers, and other settlers. Responding to the demands of agricultural interests, state legislatures used state powers to destroy many animals, especially the larger predators. Bounties were placed on a wide variety of predator birds, large cats, bears and so on. Professional hunters could earn a substantial income through several sources, including ranchers' and legislatures' bounties, and sales of hides, feathers, and meat.

Meat and market hunters attacked large herds and flocks with an unprecedented vengeance. Modern technology provided the wherewithal, especially shotguns (some with immense bores that fired several ounces of shot) and high powered, long-range, telescope-sighted rifles. One market hunter could kill more carrier pigeons, swans, bison, ducks, deer, antelope, or elk in a single day than an army might have killed in a week heretofore. Almost overnight the large groupings of birds and mammals began to disappear.

Still, man was civilized enough to try to stop the slaughter before the last of each species died. He provided laws to end the slaughter and monies to restore living and nesting areas. He undertook to develop new educational specialties that studied game management. He volunteered to pay taxes to support wildlife restoration. He gave up lands suitable to other human uses so that wildlife might survive.

But many of the problems of game preservation were unrelated to hunting. Alien species of animals competed with native species, challenging them on their home territories. Some species could meet the challenge and others could not. Some species could adapt and coexist with urban man, some could coexist with farming and ranching, and others could not adapt to the coming of man at all. Some species demanded isolation from man and retreated into the wilderness until there was no more wilderness. Some, such as the carrier pigeon, could exist only in large groupings, and they disappeared. In some cases species vanished, following a hard and fast rule of evolution that species that cannot adapt must die. This rule was laid down by nature before there was man on earth, and it has been followed even to this day. Some artificial measures have prolonged the lives of some species, well beyond the day nature may have decreed for obsolescence.

The encroachment of man, the pollution of his factories and his chemicals, and the general human conquest of nature have all contributed to the demise of animal species. Listed in nearly all catalogues of explanations for the decline of numbers of endangered species as the two principal causes are encroachment on the habitat and pollution of the living and nesting areas. The chemical DDT has been a godsend in the control of certain diseases, but it shows up in birds' eggs, causing these to be barren or to split before hatching time. Man has converted land to his use as cities and farms, and some animals cannot or will not cohabit.

Few, if any, species have been endangered by the sport hunter. Most endangered species that have been purposefully killed beyond the level that the species will tolerate have been killed by meat or hide hunters, not by sportsmen. Others have been hunted down as constituting a danger to man. Conversely, man the hunter has contributed significantly to the restoration of species and to the protection of their nesting and breeding grounds.

Those who oppose hunting are frequently ignorant of what constitutes a hunt. While the term "hunter" is shared by meat and bounty and hide hunters on the one hand, and game and sport hunters on the other, there is precious little the two groups have in common. A sport hunter will probably use the hide and meat, and, occasionally, mount the head or other portion of the animal, and he may collect a bounty on a kill. But he hunts for pleasure, although he may also desire to have the meat for his own or other's use. But his object is not directly a profit, and he hunts the elusive game that offers him a challenge. He will not endanger a species, and he will frequently contribute to its propagation.

The sport hunter would not be interested in the whale, the seal, and the walrus. He would not pursue the dolphin. He was not interested in seeking out the dodo bird or similar exotic but indefensible species. He would rarely be interested in killing in mass, choosing only to kill that which presents a challenge.

His approach to hunting provides him with a profound respect for nature, and this, in turn, prompts him to develop an ethic which he must follow because of his character. He has concluded, as reasonable men might, that there is no moral or providential proscription against hunting. He will treat game with a certain respect, not because they have rights as animals, but because there is a special relationship, a natural order of things between man and his quarry. There are rules of the hunt and he, if he is a moral person, is compelled by conscience to obey.

Only in the Eastern religions of a pantheistic type is man reduced to the level of animals. These religions suggest that there is a necessary and conclusive relationship between man, animals, and the deity, and one may return to this world as a snail, a slug, a lion, or an elephant. In such a theology one may conclude that hunting is wrong, but this is not the general religion of the West.

The Judaeo-Christian theology teaches that man is qualitatively different from the animals. He is the pinnacle of Creation. There is a special relationship man shares with his God because man was made in the image and likeness of God. He is as much different from the animals below him as the monkey is from the stone. He was not an accidental product of an undirected, random evolutionary process; he is God's high ally.

Western theology in all its mainstream branches and divisions teaches that God gave man the right to name the animals. That implies that man is given dominion and control over the wild kingdom, and that he may use them for fulfillment of his needs and wants. The use of meat, bones, and hides is sufficient, as is the pleasure associated and derived from the hunt. Man was charged by Genesis with subduing the earth to his own use. One portion of that may licitly involve hunting.

Therefore, we must reject those arguments which hold that animals have God-given rights, or that animals have immortal souls. These arguments simply do not hold up under close examination in the context of standard Western theology. No limitation on hunting can be fabricated that is predicated on animal theology.

Beyond the immediate theological implications of alleged animal rights we have a second major concern about hunting stated in terms of the natural rights of these creatures. Again, there is a certain necessary relation to theology as animal or human rights are generally viewed as given by Nature (read, Nature's God), or placed in Nature by God. We then speak of animal rights as necessary to the liberation of animals. But one classic, mainstream definition of man is a rights-possessing animal. It is precisely in his attachment to rights that man becomes man and is not an animal. Were animals also to have rights, such a definition, following John Locke and

Thomas Jefferson, would be meaningless. Of all the beings in this world, traditional natural rights thinkers tie only man to a concept of rights.

The attempts by Teilhard de Chardin and Albert Schweitzer and others of the modern synthesis of theology and evolutionary theory must fail when they reduce man to a position of being merely the highest creation to date. They eventually flounder in the sea of pantheism. They come eventually to reject traditional Christian dogmas, thereby invalidating their noble attempts to bring science and theology to a confluence.

In the final analysis only the state has the right, albeit, power, to attempt to prevent hunting. Organized religion, theological teachings and ethical considerations may suffice to prevent some from hunting, but they lack the power to compel men to stop hunting. A true state has sufficient power to compel men to do many things, but at least the democratic state cannot ordinarily compel when men are unwilling.

There is a legal right to hunt. The law had been misused in ages past to reserve hunting for the few, but, overall, hunting rights are rights of men. As rights broadened generally so they broadened specifically, as concerns us here, to permit hunting by most or all men. Even when state power proscribed hunting of some species by commoners, it still permitted hunting of other species by common men.

The state's power to enforce conservation is clearly recognized in civilized nations. Meat and market hunters may violate such laws, but the sport hunter supports them out of self-interest. That is the best reason generally for men to support the law. Hunters know that future hunts, not only by themselves, but by ensuing generations is guaranteed only when strict conservation is practiced. Thus, the hunter will obey and respect hunting laws that limit seasons, close seasons entirely, or limit kills.

I conclude that, overall, the state may not licitly close public lands entirely to hunting. Certain safety and protective steps, such as requiring a guide to be present, may be taken. Beyond the legality there is the practical side. Unlimited herds die of starvation, as in the Table Mesa, when set up in unnatural conditions. Hunters are employed and paid by tax monies to kill (and waste) surplus game. There is a compelling practical reason to permit hunting. The guides and other costs can be borne by hunters, not the general public.

Finally, I see the right to hunt protected under the unenumerated rights contained in Amendment IX to the Constitution. Other unspecified rights are now so protected, and so also may hunting be incorporated and protected. There is a substantial volume of evidence that suggests that the Supreme Court of the United States could recognize the right to hunt. Presently, the right to hunt may be placed in that category Locke spoke of wherein men claim a natural right but the state has yet to take notice of that right. But, as Locke would say, that makes the right so claimed no less real.

Hunting has proved to be of incidental, but substantial, value to the state. The 1966 Arthur D. Little Report to The U.S. Army on the National Board to Promote Rifle practice concluded that shooting sports, hunting included, provide the armed forces with a significant reservoir of trained manpower. Such men make better soldiers and are more efficient as soldiers. They shoot better, they fire their weapons in combat more frequently, and they suffer fewer casualties than untrained troops. The United States Supreme Court in 1939 ruled that states (and, presumably, the federal government) may not act in such a way with gun laws as to prevent the maintenance of this reservoir of skilled manpower. Presumably, this reservoir could be filled by hunters, and thus their right would be protected under the Second Amendment to the United States Constitution.

On the Pleasures of Hunting

The greatest Spanish philosopher of modern times is, without a reasonable doubt, Jose Ortega y Gasset (1883-1955). Born of a patrician family in Madrid, Ortega had earned his doctorate in philosophy by the time he was twenty-one. He studied at the great universities of Germany for nearly a decade before returning to teach at the University of Madrid. One of the most prolific modern writers, he is known for both the clarity of thought and the beauty of the prose he used to formulate and express his ideas. No cloistered academic, Ortega was an active politician, and he was an avid hunter. While in exile from his home nation he completed an essay in honor of his friend Edward, Count Yebes, which was included as a preface to Yebes' book on his worldwide hunting experiences, *Twenty Years a Big-Game Hunter.* Ortega's essay was written in Lisbon, Portugal, in 1942, and published in Yebes' book in 1943. The Yebes book was an unusually good and interesting collection of hunting stories, but there was a special quality to Ortega's introductory essay. The introduction under the title *Meditations on Hunting* was reprinted in Spanish by itself three times (1947, 1949, 1960) and was translated into German (three editions, 1954, 1959, 1966), Dutch (1964), Japanese (1966) and English (1972). No essay states the hunter's point of view more precisely, clearly, or beautifully than Ortega's writing.

Ortega's neo-Kantian philosophy led him to conclude that man was a product of himself and his total circumstances. "I am but half of my total personality," he said. "The circumstances and environment around me are "the other half of my personality." One does not simply co-exist with his environment-experience matrix; one who is truly human necessarily interacts with these things. Man's activities are at least half of his human existence. Without human interaction with things, one cannot become self-fulfilled. Activity is life, the dynamic interaction of mutually dependent self and the things around man. Our lives are but missions of self-expression, self-becoming, carried out with all that surrounds us. Ortega's theory of knowledge is known to us as "perspectivism"; that is, the world can only be known from one's own specific point of view.

1

Our own individuality is guaranteed by the unique set of perspectives which each of necessity develops.

Throughout Ortega's many writings, he speaks of "life" and "vitality" as essential qualities man must understand and develop in order to become truly human. These terms may be connected to the more traditional term of "practical reason." Vitality is interrelated not with mere biological vitality, but with man's mission of self-creation. Man's nature is unimportant, perhaps non-existent; what is important is man's history. Man's quest is not for his nature, but for a drama in which he partakes as an actor in a necessarily vital and dynamic way. Vital man freely chooses the play(s) in which he partakes. There is neither fatalism nor determinism in Ortega · Man's mission is not one of historical importance in shaping all history; it is a personal one of each individual man working out his own being, his own destiny, along the lines that best suit him.

Our lives are always bounded by and threatened by cultural insecurities. That was the great message of Ortega's internationally acclaimed *The Revolt of the Masses* (1930). Society as a whole, and great men specifically, are always struggling against perpetual crisis, trying to sustain some semblance of order in the face of impending barbarism. These desperate measures of a desperate society constitute human culture. The masses of men must look to an aristocracy of merit to provide some direction, to be a beacon of hope in a world bordering on chaos. Although we speak of both the equality of men and the soul of societies, both are myths which have threatened our culture and made its battles more difficult. All things that are collective are subhuman and subversive of man's struggle to know true nature. These mass collectives Ortega calls "quasi-nature."

Against this background Ortega develops his theory of the pleasures of hunting. Hunting is an escape that is necessary for man as a form of preservation of his sanity. It is a necessary diversion that allows man to skip over "quasi-nature" and commune most directly with nature. It is a pursuit that man alone follows as an avocation, as recreation. It is one of the most highly individualistic activities of men. It is man alone against the wild animals, in a unique situation not repeated elsewhere in all of nature. It is one activity for which there is no substitute. There is no possible substitution through simulation. One either hunts, or one does not hunt. It permits no middle ground.

The hunt has a precise and definable content. One does not hunt with a camera, for the mere taking of a picture cannot complete the act. One does not hunt without a weapon. One does not hunt without thinking of the kill. There is to be no moderizing of the term so as to permit a broad definition of acts that may be included under the term hunting. One cannot permit the prostitution of the idea by removing one of its many essential elements, such as the taking of animal life.

The types of hunting are but two: sport and essential. Paleolithic man hunted out of necessity. Occasionally, in unique circumstances, modern man may have to hunt to survive. Such hunting differs little from the hunting done by animals, carnivores who must hunt to survive. Man only improved on the methodology of the hunt when he added weapons and tools to the essential hunt. An essential hunter may not hunt differently from the sport hunter, given equal technologies available to both kinds of hunters. A primitive man hunted with the weapons that were, to him, state-of-the-art technology. A modern man, thrown into unusual situations which require him to kill to survive, will also hunt with the best weapons available to him. In either case, if he has the leisure time available, he may chose to decorate his weapons or to create aesthetically pleasing weapons that may not be the best weapons from the viewpoint of practical use.

The quintessential feature of modern man, at least since the neolithic age, is that he need not hunt for survival, save for the very unusual and occasional circumstances of survival. It has become a universal and impassioned sport that belongs within the general repertory of human enjoyment. We hunt now to amuse ourselves, not to survive. It makes no difference that men hunt now with a rifle or with a handgun and that other, earlier men had only the spear, or the bow and arrow. Indeed, modern man may eschew his most recent technology and may choose to hunt with obsolete or obsolescent weapons, such as muzzle-loading or flintlock rifles, or the bow and arrow.

While men hunt animals to kill or capture them, it is not the exclusive, or even necessarily the primary purpose of hunting. Man as man precedes the hunt. Man is man before he is hunting man. He hunts in order to complete the chain of "I and my environment." Since this relationship between man and his environment culminated before we could speak of advances in weapons technology, the idea of applied and modern technology is transcended by the idea of the hunt. Man hunts, irrespective of his choice of weapons, because he wishes to enter into this most unique of all truly human relationships with the wild animals, and through them, with nature.

The idea of hunting transcends any idea of progress. Man hunts in order to kill or capture an animal, and this is true regardless of the choice of weapons or the motivation behind the hunt. The classification of motivations is of passing and academic interest, but the motivations do not change the essential characteristics of the hunt itself.

Hunting requires a certain kind of confrontation between man and the animal. He is seeking one or a few of a species for his personal use in whatever way he chooses to use these animals. It is unlike war in that the hunter does not seek to annihilate the species, nor to destroy all or most of their numbers. Indeed, this kind of destruction would be counter-productive since, after the hunt was completed, there could be no future hunts.

After man developed the technology to destroy all animals of a certain species he was obliged to develop certain restraints on the impulse to use that technology; otherwise no more hunting would be possible. The hunter who would machine-gun all elephants to destroy their kind would certainly not be hunting; nor would a person who poisoned a water hole to kill all roebucks be classified as a hunter.

Indeed, as man developed and chose to use more effective weapons he chose also to limit himself in the pursuit of game. A hunter with a bow and arrow had to be a better hunter than one who equipped himself with a very powerful rifle mounted with a powerful telescopic sight. After a certain point the hunt could degenerate into nothing more than a slaughter of game. Thus, in one way, the choice of weapons and devices can be said to alter, even prevent, the true hunt. One who fired bursts of automatic rifle fire into the forest, with the hope that a bullet may strike and kill a deer, cannot be said to be hunting. All that massive applications of destructive capabilities prove is that man is rationally superior to the animals. With too great an application of power, man has become a destroyer, not a hunter. It is difficult to state precisely when hunting ceases to be hunting and precisely when it becomes mere slaughter. But it is clear that the animal adversary will not improve its techniques of survival over and against such massive applications of advanced technology.

When man ceases to be a hunter, he has harmed himself far more than he has harmed nature or the animal kingdom. He has degraded human activity of the highest order and has made it an activity unworthy of mankind. He has cut himself off from that essential communion with nature, from the pursuit of man against the wiles of the natural creature. He has placed himself in the same situation as the person who kills off houseflies with an aerosol spray; and certainly that cannot be called hunting.

Hunting implies a basic and necessary inequality between hunter and hunted. In the animal world the lion is superior to the deer; the cat is superior to the mouse; and the bird is superior to the insect. When we speak of equality of power we are really talking about combat or war. When we speak of hunting, we do not imagine our prey to be equal to ourselves in power or intelligence. Indeed, we would be extremely hard-pressed to find even one example in nature of a less gifted or weaker animal hunting a superior foe. Man may pursue or chase his fellow man, he may make war on him, and he may take him on in single combat, but he cannot hunt him.

War and combat involve mutual aggression. There is an equality between the participants that is not duplicated in the hunt. Here, we cannot speak of "war" between animals and humans in a reasonable sense. Man may deceive himself into thinking that he can combat a bear or make war on deer; but this extends our reasonable definitions beyond the breaking point.

No one expects the deer to be able to counterattack the hunter. The hunter does not expect even a large and powerful animal, such as a lion or a bear, to have a chance of preventing the hunter from killing it. Such is not the nature of the hunt.[1]

Neither do we think of the hunt as a kind of nearly even contest between man and the animals. In Ortega's native Spain, and in much of the Spanish-speaking world, bullfighting is a popular sport. The bull, indeed, has some chance of killing or maiming the hunter. At times cruel men may pit a human against a stronger and more powerful animal without providing the human contestant with a weapon, or by giving the human only a simple and inferior weapon such as a dagger. Such activities were part of the late Roman gladiatorial games. Such actions are neither hunting nor combat.

Hunting requires that the pursued be a wild animal. One finds no pleasure in slaughtering a cow, because the cow cannot possibly be a worthy foe. It is a degenerate animal, devoid of much of its instincts that, at one time, might have allowed it to be a worthy subject of a hunt. Early on in history, man discovered what animals could be easily taken into captivity and bred there for indiscriminate slaughter whenever meat was required. It is possible that the ancestors of the cow and other domesticated animals would never have been worthy subjects of a hunt. By the same token, many animals that have existed, or which still exist, could not be hunted. These could be gathered up and slaughtered; they offered no element of evasion. Early man, who slaughtered out of necessity, no doubt preferred to slaughter when meat was scarce or especially needed; he apparently preferred to hunt when he could afford that luxury. Primitive man slaughtered the giant sloth, which apparently could be taken at will; modern man gathers and slaughters the giant tortoises which provide little resistence. When some animal life led a sheltered existence without natural predators, it survived; but when that life was challenged, it disappeared. Such was the case of the giant dodo bird. It was slaughtered easily and no hunt was involved, either for man or for the man-induced wild pigs and dogs.

To be worthy of a human hunt, the hunted must present something of a challenge. To early man the challenge was presented to his wits and his instincts as well as to his primitive weapons. As technology negated our need for strong senses and instincts, we used our more sophisticated weapons to retain parity. The great, enchanting, enticing thing about the hunt is the simple fact that it may not be successful. The game may elude us; the animals may escape our best efforts; the animals may thwart our most advanced techniques and aids. If we choose to seek out and destroy a cow in the field, our probability of success is nearly 100%. If we poison a water hole, our chance of failing to wind up with a dead animal is nearly zero. But if we must rely on our own ability, there is some considerable chance that we will be unsuccessful; success is not automatic.

The joy and pleasure of hunting is only slightly diminished if we are not successful. We should have enjoyed the pursuit. If we have challenged a game animal and failed to kill or capture it, we will still have had the fond memories of a hunt. We may lose the joy of hunting if we are constantly unsuccessful, but ordinarily we enjoy hunting because there is some chance of success and some of failure. Boredom occurs when the hunt is always a failure or always a success. Neither our superiority nor our inferiority to the hunted may be absolute.

The hunt begins when man has chosen to pursue an animal; it ends when he has captured or killed his prey. It may be terminated when the game has eluded him, or when, for a variety of other reasons, he has chosen to end it. But, we must return to, and reaffirm, an essential point: the hunt is not completed if we see, photograph, or merely observe the animal. That may be called stalking the animal, but it negates the necessary culmination of the successful hunt. The unsuccessful hunt has terminated because man was unable to kill or capture the animal. A hunt which stops short of killing or capturing the prey is aborted. In short, the only true and natural hunt seeks to kill or capture the quarry.

The hunt involves a confrontation between two sets of instincts. For the hunter, the instinct is to kill. For the hunted, the instinct is to elude the hunter and thus avoid being killed. For man to have a suitable subject to hunt, the animal must have its natural and unimpeded instincts. For man, this is impossible. But the hunt reinforces and keeps alive man's most basic instincts. He may technically augment his own instincts and compensate for lost instincts; but he must, nonetheless, have as an essential part of the hunt his best and most basic human instincts. There would be little of man's instincts used in merely killing game that has been captured and released for his slaughter, as in live pigeon shooting. Again, there would be little of the hunt left in killing of game under unnatural surroundings. Indeed, one can say that the killing of game under unnatural conditions would be counterproductive to maintaining the hunting instinct.

If it were otherwise, man could merely shoot at cardboard game targets; he could practice his art in a shooting gallery. But man cannot truly hunt by merely shooting at targets. He cannot commune with nature by perfecting his marksmanship on the range. In short, anything that smacks of unnatural conditions places man in confrontation with "quasi-nature"—that is, that which he seeks to overcome and avoid precisely by hunting.

The most instructive and useful form of hunting would occur in the most natural, and the least disturbed, settings. The truest form of hunting would occur when man would be least impeded by human instruments, such as plowed fields or fences. The animal, in its turn, has an instinctive response, a pre-conditioned nature, that prepares it for the hunter. It best fulfills its role as the hunted in that which is closest to its long history, closest to that which nature has prepared it over untold generations. The hunt thus does not arrive at the animal by chance; it is an event whose coming was foretold by years of preconditioning long before the hunter came to hunt. The animal loses its chances for survival, not by being hunted, but by being placed in unnatural conditions for which its preconditioning did not prepare it adequately. Within the reasonable limits Ortega has set for the hunt, each measure taken by the hunter is countered naturally by the hunted, so long as its environment is not altered.

Such a partnership, with clearly defined role expectations between man and nature, is unheard of elsewhere. Each has been preconditioned to its role by thousands, even millions, of years. Ortega argues that no artificial, that is, "quasi-natural," relationship between man and the animals can be fabricated, that would create a better reciprocity between the two forms of life. Those things which man hunts will be limited in some way with or without man. The hunted will always be the hunted, with the only choice being that made by man of who shall hunt. Nothing will change in the animal kingdom if man chooses not to hunt; the animals will retain their instinctive abilities to give man a chase, whether he chooses to hunt them or not. They will still have capacities to resist being captured and killed after man ceases to hunt them, just as they were preconditioned to avoid the hunter before man hunted them.

Man can choose freely to reject his instincts and to refrain from hunting. He can repudiate this natural relationship and abrogate the partnership that was foreordained before man became man. It will affect only man, not the animals. He can remove the joy of the hunt, but he cannot change the predator to prey on nature about him.

It is with more than just a passing interest that Ortega notes that man has the broadest range of prey of any of the hunting species. There are many animals that can present a challenge to man the hunter. The elusiveness of a smaller game provides the interest here. The tools that man has created have provided him with the means to hunt the largest and most dangerous animals in the world. Man has found that nearly every species of animal life can provide him with some sort of challenge in the hunt. He eschews only those species that have not learned to be prey, as was the case with the dodo birds. He rejects those which he has domesticated, although the wild (hence, natural) forms of many of these, such as the wild pig or goat, provide him with the necessary challenge. As man's prowess increases, and his natural instincts are rekindled, perhaps redeveloped, he chooses, if possible, to hunt the most elusive species

The true hunter wishes always, to increase his skills so that he may pursue the most developed and conditioned of the animal world. This would be natural to man; it would show that, if he were successful in the hunt, he had developed, insofar as possible, the natural instincts and skills of natural man—that is, man the hunter.

Historic man has always been faced with a relative scarcity of game. Ortega put a great deal of effort into trying to establish just how scarce game was in times beginning with the Neolithic Age. He concluded that even in the late years of the Paleolithic Age the supply of game had diminished. When he was able to use archaeological findings, he calculated that even early man had found too little game, and he concluded reasonably that this paucity of huntable animals had forced some changes in man's eating and hunting habits. By the time he was able to pick up recorded hunts, mankind was only a few hundred years away from the birth of Christ. The Graeco-Roman historians tell us that several things had happened. Gamelands within what was then the civilized world were generally reserved for kings and nobility. Daily or annual bag limits had been established. Species were imported from distant lands to augment the local supplies of game animals. Kings and nobles frequently journeyed long distances for a first class hunt. Private domains were created, much like modern pay hunting grounds, to contain both native and exotic species of game. Hunting by commoners, almost everywhere, became a major crime. Kings expropriated to themselves the right to own and control game, although ordinarily the game itself was said not to be the subject to ownership, for animals existed *ferrae naturae*.

Ortega concluded that herein lay the great paradox of hunting. All men, or nearly all, wished to hunt. For all to hunt there must be quantities of game animals. But if game is very plentiful there is no great interest in the hunt, for, even with primitive weapons, the hunter's chance of killing an animal was great—so great, perhaps, that the challenge was absent. He thus assumed that, for all intents and purposes, there had always been a scarcity of game, and that there always would be such a scarcity. Further, he concluded that even if there were no scarcity man would generally seek out those few species that were scarce. In short, to suggest that the hunt would be a success unless something very unusual were to happen was to suggest as well that hunting had lost its romance. He also believed that if game were more plentiful, the animals would lose much of their ability to elude hunters. There would then be no reason for nature to implant such strong survival instincts in the animals, and thus the hunt would lose its challenges.

Ortega is suggesting here that as the numbers of a species decrease, the awareness of survival—unconsciously developed of course—would make the surviving few more able to utilize complex countermeasures. In one sense this suggests improvement of instinct in the species; but, in a more correct context, it merely suggests that those surviving members of a species are the ones with the strongest and most developed instincts. This would enhance the value of that species as a desirable prey and thus force man to become an even more able hunter. This then served man and animal alike.

By the time we can find hunting in recorded history, man had become aware of the great value of conservation. This was a two-pronged fork, for it applied to the total exclusion of most men, and it required even kings to exercise caution. Men knew nothing then of the scientific breeding of wild animals, or of their creation and rearing in artificial surroundings. They knew precious little of moving some species to new areas; indeed, in the latter case, man in modern times did this in nearly every case, without planning and, of course, with often catastrophic results. So the most man could do was to try to cut back on hunting for a time, relying on natural selection and natural regeneration to restock game lands.

Throughout recorded history we find that chronicles mention especially noteworthy times or places when or where game was in abundance. Ortega finds especially interesting those which relate how a certain king would spend a great amount of time, perhaps several days, searching for an especially elusive quarry. He concluded that one great charm of the hunt came in building up to that one splendid moment when the prey was sighted. It was then the skill of the hunter pitted against the survival instincts of the animal. Quick, man thought, I must respond in a split second and with deadly accuracy, for this moment may never be repeated. That kind of thrill was possible only if game were scarce. It stands in stark contrast to the simple act of going out to slaughter meat for the table, whether done among domesticated animals, or among plentiful deer in a king's private forest.

So coveted was the privilege of hunting that wars were fought over game lands, not so they might provide basic life support for starving masses, but so they might provide sport for the few. Ortega argues that such wars for privileged hunting had developed at the dawn of time, and were certainly not a modern invention. Early on, he believed, man had developed a hunter class, far more exclusive than such simple prerequisites as being a member of the tribe and being male. He accepted without a single doubt that rank and standing were wholly interrelated with hunting prowess and hunting success.

Only rarely in recorded history, or even in recent pre-history, has game been found in significant quantities. North America stands out as the great exception. Here ideal climatic conditions, soil, nutritional opportunities combined with a tiny, almost insignificant, technologically backward people to cause game to flourish in unprecedented numbers. Ortega believed that this unusual and unexpected circumstance disrupted man's European hunting traditions. Men at all levels of social standing hunted, nay, slaughtered the animals. Most lost their sense of propriety and proportion and killed and wasted the native game. This, combined with man's technology to kill in numbers unthought of by the Amerindians, led to the decimation of the great herds of game. Finally, man brought with him from the Old Country the plow that broke the plains and the axe that denuded the forest, and the natural habitat was gone forever.

Only after a more normal (i.e., normal to the Europeans) condition was brought about, a condition of scarcity of game, did man stop the slaughter and begin hunting again. But, by then, some game animals had disappeared. Others were brought back from total annihilation only by significant applications of new game management technologies. Scarcity and restrictions on hunting, and the conditions of normalcy, allowed man to emerge once again as hunter, rather than slaughterhouse operator. The true thrill of hunting was restored and, so long as it was uninterrupted by the further imposition of unnatural conditions, the hunt would go on endlessly.

When game is scarce, it develops a number of countermeasures to avoid being killed or captured. One of the most effective ways to avoid man is to hide from him. Most hunted species have developed very elaborate ways to elude detection, frequently by blending in with the scenery. Since modern cultural man is not natural man, his once keen senses have diminished in power. Modern man will walk right over a rabbit, or within a foot or two of a grouse, and never notice it. Modern man needed a partner in the hunt.

The partner man needed was the dog. Ortega believed that the dog first approached man, probably attracted to his castoffs from the hunt. In any event, the compact between man and dog has been one of the great symbiotic relationships of all times. Man offered the dog his shelter and protection. The dog offered man assistance in the hunt. Each offered the other love, affection, and loyalty. In return for some portions of meat, the dog assisted man in his hunts. Even after long domestication, the dog has retained its natural instincts. The dog has undergone radical change through selective breeding, so that various breeds assist man in different ways, and through a variety of hunting experiences. But man established synergistic relationships with other creatures, including birds, such as the falcon, and such highly improbable, hunting partners as the panther.

This special relationship of two animal species to one another is not found elsewhere in nature. In all other symbiotic relationships, the host and the guest tolerate one another but do not communicate or express feelings or sentiments toward one another. Each has an existence of its own, and that life pattern interfaces with another life pattern. But there is no compact, no expressed relationship.

The idea of a pet is, of course, tied up with the hunt. Man, at least primitive man, would have been an unlikely subject for a mere master-to-pet relationship. He would have had no time for a lap dog. Food was generally too scarce to share with a mere object. The hunting partner had to earn his way daily. But all of this does not preclude the possibility of having a strong secondary relationship that especially benefitted man. The dog became a true, natural intermediary with nature. It was not a mere "quasi-natural" obstacle between man and nature. It was his direct and vital link with nature itself; and it resulted from hunting.

As a link with nature, the dog helped to regenerate within man a natural, basic and instinctive hunting pattern. The dog was close to man, not just on the hunt, but always. There was a reciprocal exchange of articulated hunting patterns, again, the omnipresent and vital link between man and nature that man cannot establish by himself. A catalyst, an active transmittal agent is mandated, and that is the role the dog fulfilled. But, to reiterate Ortega's point, such would not have been possible without the hunt. Man would have lost, inexorably and irretrievably, his point of contact with nature, his window to the real and natural world.

The end of the hunt is the kill. For Ortega, the idea of "hunting" is impossible without the idea of taking an animal's life. Anything less is not hunting. Man aims for the thrill of the hunt itself, but the necessary, culminating step is the kill or the capture. Man does not kill because he wishes to kill; rather, he kills because it is the only logical thing to do. The chase itself is something other than a hunt if man does not finalize the process by taking the animal's life.

If the kill itself were the quintessential part of the hunt, man could avoid the trials, tribulations and uncertainties of the hunt merely by slaughtering a cow or hog. But it is something more than that. It is, for Ortega, the one thing that finalizes the hunt and gives it its character.

Man alone can give nobility and respect to his prey. The ideas of nobility and respectability are events which occur to the hunted as a result of a completed hunt, that is, one which results in a kill. Man changes and lowers the character, and alters and lessens the nobility of the game animal if he chooses not to kill it. He is saying, no, I do not respect you, and therefore I will not kill you. When he comes on a weak or sick animal, he may fail to offer it the character of nobility, and, thus, will not kill it. But, Ortega argues, the great and magnificent animal cries out for nobility and respect. The hunter is thus compelled to shoot it. If he does not, it is man who will suffer, for he has rejected the animal. The animal itself will never know, but man, on his own, will have rejected the natural end of the hunt. He will have contravened the natural order. Man is the hunter, and the prey is the hunted. For each to be truly natural, each must fill out its expected and natural role. Anything less is sacrilege, a sin against nature. In a word, Ortega concluded that man does not hunt in order to kill; conversely, he kills in order that he can be said to have hunted. The beast is reconciled to its fate; it has fulfilled its duty if it has proven to be a true adversary, a worthy subject for the hunt. Thus, it is sufficient that man kills the hunted.

The hunt has been an event in and of itself, a hedonistic adventure, a joyous experience. It has brought man into direct, basic, and natural contact with true, unadulterated nature. Death to the mighty beast is essential precisely because without it there has been no hunt and thus all else has been reduced to meaninglessness.

Man's rationality gives man a choice in killing. He has, up until the moment of the kill, pitted his intelligence against animal instincts to survive and escape. Hunting is a contest between the rationality of man and the instincts of his intended prey. Ortega held that man's rationality and the animal's instincts operated in much the same fields, but at different levels, and with different sources and outlets. Man can observe and learn from the animal, that is, he can study its habits and use his intelligence to outwit the beast. The animal, for its part, uses its natural cunning and instinctive responses and sharper senses to elude man.

Man can spend only a tiny portion of his total time on earth learning to hunt. He can practice his theoretical skills only a few days a year. The animal lives with its instincts constantly and has no diversions, for survival and the animal are one. Man, for the most part, has forgotten his hunting and has, through civilization, lost his instincts and keen senses. But the contest is nonetheless loaded toward man. The animal may prove a worthy subject for the hunt, but it can never compete with man on equal footing. Man may choose—indeed, ought to choose—to narrow the gap between him and his quarry, but he can never equalize the two. The closer man operates to the animal level—that is, the more he repudiates technology that weights the hunt toward man—the better the hunt, and the more profitable the experience will be for him. If we are to profit from the hunt, if we are to learn what we have unfortunately forgotten, we must throw ourselves fully, wholly, and heroically into the hunt. We must operate as close to nature as our humanity will permit. We will never again return to the hunt without our weapons, but we can make certain that our weapons are not wholly dominant. If I am to become myself, that is I plus the environment I have chosen, then I must let the hunt become me; I must reach out and embrace it fully. I cannot move away from the kill; I cannot become too dependent on my tools; and I cannot refuse to attempt to recapture my natural self.

I do not hunt in order to do something else. I do not hunt, says Ortega, to enjoy nature. I enjoy nature because, through hunting, I have become a part of it. I do not hunt so that I may enjoy the sounds of my dogs barking on the trails; I enjoy the sound of the hounds because I am hunting. I do not kill game because I enjoy the act of taking a life; I take that life so that I have satisfied the requirements of the hunt. I do not create the requirements, the vital and indispensable elements of the natural order. I understand them, I accept them, and I live within their stated limitations. If I become a law unto myself, I have broken the rules, and my existential becoming, I and my chosen environment, suffer as a logical and necessary consequence. I have posited my existence within an ordered and highly hierarchical natural universe by communing as I am required to communicate, that is, by hunting.

I may choose not to hunt. That is a free choice. But Ortega argues there are no natural substitutes for hunting. The artificial substitutes are unsatisfactory. They are only "quasi-natural" and form a barrier between myself and nature, a barrier I have sought to avoid precisely by hunting. Thus the non-hunter is an unfulfilled man. He cannot recapture his basic nature, and is, predator and carnivore, in another way.

Hunting provides the one logical escape for man's frustrations in a culturally degenerate society. While all the world is threatening collapse around me, I can find one solace, one natural outlet, one reasonable escape, that which comes only through hunting.

Ortega argues as well that hunting is a possible outlet for man's aggression. It is a substitute for war and inter-human violence. Man is aggressive because he is naturally a hunter. That is a necessary attribute of a hunter. He is not docile, because that is the trait of the hunted, and that is precisely the opposite of man's position. War and violence have been costly, unfortunate and unsatisfying substitutes for hunting. The timid among us might never have been satisfactory hunters. Early on, they would have been removed from the hunting elite. That would be the net result of natural selection. For man to have survived as a hunter he would have to have had inbred a strong desire to aggressive behavior. Docile behavior would have been bred out, perhaps by denying women to the timid, perhaps by denying food to the meek in times of scarcity. The strong, the aggressive, survived.

Man has not changed in the short period of time we call history or civilization. Man ought not to change, says Ortega. Indeed, man ought to recapture his fundamental impulses, his instincts if he can, and his keen senses if he is able. This would be the natural "becoming" of each man, working out his own personal history. Man cannot, and never will be able to return to the state of Paleolithic man. He has and will continue to develop culture as a bulwark against his return to savagery and barbarism. But he also has the natural side, man the hunter.

Man the Hunter

The twentieth century has brought into existence more new sciences than man could have conceived of in earlier times. But the explosion of knowledge into fragmented fields has made cooperation among these disciplines all but impossible until very recently. We were far too busy dividing up knowledge to be bothered sharing this vast accumulation of information.

With the advent of cooperation among many and diverse fields, and with the syntheses suggested by more popular writers in unspecialized books created largely for lay persons, we have come to some very startling conclusions about ourselves and the world in which we live. Nowhere is this more true than in the general area of the prehistory of man. Almost daily, we discover in some of the most unlikely places in this world, things that, when properly interpreted, lead us to surprising and new conclusions about man as he lived not just thousands, but millions of years ago.

It would be well to state certain basics that I have assumed as starting points, things about the nature of man and the study of man, things that will undoubtedly color my presentation here. First, I do accept the idea of the creation of the world *ex nihilo*—that is, out of nothing. This suggests that I accept a wholly powerful and fully transcendent God, a deity so great that we can conceive little about him. We must, therefore, merely state a few things about the Godhead in negative ways, e.g., that he is unlimited, boundless, and that he can do all things not involving a contradiction.

Second, I believe that there is and always was a divine plan, carried out by providence, that function of God that, moment by moment, sustains the world in existence, constantly renewing the Creation. As a part of the grand scheme of things, God placed certain innate knowledge within each of us, and within all plant and animal life as well. This plan is thus constantly unfolding upon itself changing and altering reality day by day. Nothing happens within this plan without a reason, and God permits all to happen, tying it to his design in ways and by methods generally incomprehensible to us.

Third, I believe that man has stated in his feeble way certain things that are, within our human limits, generally true. One such set of laws are commonly known as Darwin's evolutionary theory. Charles Darwin, like all who attempt to fathom God's laws and plans, saw through the proverbial glass but darkly. But he was a giant on whose shoulders rests the evolutionary sciences of the present day. Others have offered reasonable corollaries and hypotheses to augment the Darwinian theories, and many of these concern the nature of man.

In contradistinction to today's highly behavioral sciences I do not believe that we can wholly modify or predict man's behavior. Man is not simply putty in the hands of the social manipulator. His activity is basically predictable in many ways, although not determined in a final way, because we have many instincts within us.

The new fields of animal sciences that have labored so long in observing the behavior of animal life inferior to man have contributed much to our basic understandings of our origins and make-up. Many of the instincts within twentieth century man have origins far back in the dawn of sentient life in the world. A baby, for example may have an innate and instinctive fear of falling that is grounded in the collective experiences of man's remote ancestors who dwelt in trees and who, thus, had good reason to fear falling.

One of my basic hypotheses here is that man is instinctively a hunter. He does not hunt for reasons of pleasure, although he has come to associate pleasure with absolute necessity. One may draw an analogy between the pleasures we have learned in the hunt and those we associate with sex. Sex, obviously, is necessary in order to procreate and to sustain our species. But we are surely permitted pleasures beyond the minimum nature requires for procreation. In the animal kingdom this is not especially the case generally, and apparently not at all the case for the female of the species. There is now abundant evidence to suggest that none but the human female can experience an orgasm.

Without the hunt man might easily go hungry, indeed, starve and die. His species could not survive. We are essentially meat eaters. Our present dietary habits have only recently, relative to the history of man on earth, been altered to include substantial quantities of vegetables. The most primitive true man might have varied his diet by including vegetables, seeds, nuts, berries and grasses, but these were the luxury items, and, of themselves, wholly incapable of sustaining human life over the long run.

Man has only recently learned to plant and harvest and store his vegetable items. For primitive man, such would have been impossible. These items would have been available only seasonally. Even then, man could not wholly count on having sufficient quantities of such items, since their appearance would have depended wholly on accidents of nature and natural regeneration.

Many vegetables had to await man's use of fire before they could be usable. Many seeds are indigestible without processing. Beans and many other vegetables must be cooked or they will be harmful to man. Others required specialized processing techniques to be useful. Still others had to be recreated by hybridization before they could be truly useful. All of this suggests considerable specialization and experimentation, activities beyond primitive man's abilities. Fire was not regularly used for cooking, for example much before fifty thousand years ago, and probably not ordinarily and commonly the property of man before 20,000 B.C.[1]

Although it may seem nearly impossible to us today, meat can be eaten raw. Indeed, raw meat may be more nutritious than cooked meat. Recent observations of Eskimoes show that these people exist for long periods of time without eating anything but raw meat. They do not incur scurvy or other similar diseases we once thought of as the natural consequence of failing to eat certain vegetables. And of course, they do not take a vitamin a day. Their raw meat diet seems to provide those essentials which are lost to us today because we cook the vitamins and other essential nutrients out of our meat. In short, our civilized way of eating meat is not the natural way of things, and, when we became modern, when we started cooking our meats, we then had to supplement our meat intake with other substances. Primitive man, like the Eskimo, followed the most basic instincts of the animal side of our human nature and ate his meat after killing it. He could thus sustain himself as a meat eater.[2]

In examining the primitive tribes of the present day we often draw wrong conclusions because we fail to understand them. First, the overwhelming majority of primitive peoples have devolved from higher civilizations of the past. They are primitive by both our own contemporary standards and by the standards of their own earlier ancestors. They have generally retained some bits and pieces of the earlier knowledge. They are not like the first men of two or so million years ago. They are also fire-possessing humans. They have learned to make, or at the worst, to capture and sustain, fire. Thus, they can cook both meats and vegetables. Further, they have learned to process, if in only the most rudimentary ways, the fruits, nuts, berries, grasses, and roots they use to sustain life. Ordinarily, their range of uses is minimal; that is, that they use only a few of the many available vegetables and the like. Others that we can process today they ignore because they have not yet learned to master these.

Further, these primitive tribes augment their diets by using meats. Some still devour even their own kind, commonly prisoners taken from alien tribes. Some still eat certain meats, or portions of certain meats, raw. Finally, because they have not mastered sufficient numbers and varieties of vegetables, but have learned to cook many meats, many primitive peoples suffer from malnutrition.

These primitive peoples of today are indeed both hunters and gatherers. They subsist on two levels of dietary intake: animal and vegetable. But they evolved, albeit very slowly, this way. This was not the most basic or primitive man. Some primitive tribes are even an additional step away from rudimentary man, having learned to plant and cultivate. This step marks them as being at least two million years away from the most primitive human being. Even those who only gather and cook are two million or so years away from base primitiveness.

The Leakey family, Louis, Mary and Richard,[3] has spent its life in some of the most undesirable parts of Africa, and through its discoveries, has moved the history of man back an almost incomprehensible amount of time. Our remote but true ancestors walked about the earth some two and a half million years ago, perhaps even more. Our knowledge of man's earliest pre-history is by no means complete today. What other amazing and highly significant discoveries that might yet be made are impossible to predict.

True man, man basically indistinguishable from our present day humans, probably did not come on the scene until about twenty-five thousand years ago. At the most, we are speaking of man as a necessarily basic meat eater until about that same time. Thus man has, at best, some twenty-five thousand years as a hunter and gatherer, as against two or more million years as a meat eater. Since he truly began to conquer agriculture only about six thousand years ago, it might be far fairer to say that he has only these six thousand years as a basically vegetable eating creature as against 2.5 million years as a carnivore.

In that vast space of time man acquired a basic need for meat, a constitutional demand for foods that only meats could provide. Drs. Michael and Sheilagh Crawford, of Britain's prestigious Nuffield Institute of Comparative Medicine, in their book, *What We Eat Today*[4] (1972), have hypothesized that the expansion of man's brain could have occurred only if he had been a meat eater. The basic fatty acids man must have as a necessary part of his central nervous system can come from only two sources: mothers' milk, or from eating animal materials. We apparently cannot wholly manufacture these from basic raw materials ourselves. We have become dependent on getting these premanufactured from other parts of the food chain, namely, from animals which have eaten basic grasses and vegetables, and which have converted these into the more complex substances our bodies require. Some animals have the necessary digestive and processing capabilities to convert these basic, simple food substances to the more complex structural fats that our central nervous systems require.

In the grand design of things the herbivores, such as cows and other grazing animals, convert the basic seeds, nuts, fruits, grasses and vegetables into the longer, more complex fat chains that do not exist in the vegetable world. These herbivores are, in turn, the food-stuffs for the carnivores which prey upon them. If it had not been a part of the grand intent that herbvivores be such intermediary units of transmittal, carnivores would either not exist, or they would have developed the capacity to alter basic vegetables into the complex structural fats man (and many other carnivores) must have.

The great crossroads was approached at the point that the common ancestor of man and the apes had to choose between becoming carnivores and herbivores. For the apes, the choice was the eating of vegetables and, consequently, a smaller, less complex brain. For man the choice was to eat meat, and thus to provide to the brain those vital fatty acids needed to alter and restructure our whole central nervous system so that it could become a higher and better system, serving to lift man above the other branches of the ape-man continuum. In man these vital fatty acids make up about 50 percent of the dry weight of the central nervous system. Without these structural fats, human life itself, at least as we have come to know of it over 2.5 million years, would have been impossible.

Obviously, there is nothing that requires that we continually partake of nothing but meat. Indeed, a single ingestion of such pre-processed fats might last us a long while. Much more research in this area will be needed. One cannot, at present, say with great certainty that present day man must eat meats at specified intervals. Neither can one say with certainty what might happen even to the offspring of several generations of strict vegetarians. But the Crawfords have surely suggested an initial need for such fats, and their research further shows that many protein-rich vegetable substances, such as soybeans, cannot provide these structural fats.

Assuming, as I have done, a grand design to man's evolution from a lower form of animal, one might conclude, reasonably, that it was planned that man's ancestors should make that great leap from animal to human by having instilled a desire to eat meat, thus providing these structural acids necessary to the growth of a complex brain. Were contemporary men to fashion evolution of their own design, they might choose to give man the capacity to convert his own structural acids directly from vegetables, thus bypassing the carnivore stage. Such an evolutionary plan would assume, then, that man would have to be dependent on the tenuous supplies of nature for vegetable matter. This, we have shown, is asking a bit much of primitive man.

Now, if we are to eat meat we have but two choices in getting that meat. We must either scavenge or we must hunt. Our primitive ancestors might, ideally, have been about 5'6'', and he might have weighed about 130 pounds. They were just beginning to master a very few weapons. They were surely not strong enough to have taken a kill away from the large predators of the day. It also seems unlikely that our ancestors were generally able to digest putrid leftovers. It was the scavenger hypothesis that was first held by those willing to admit that our primitive ancestors ate meat as a staple of their diet.

The scavenger hypothesis was most recently and persuasively challenged by Robert Ardrey in his *The Hunting Hypothesis* (1976).[5] The thesis is masterful for its simplicity and logic. If we had been unable to kill large animals known by archaeology to have been eaten by primitive man, how had we been able to take these kills away from those animals which had killed them? Ardrey supposes that most animals had not been instinctively afraid of the apes because they were herbivores. Thus, primitive man, as he evolved as a carnivore, was able to approach animals more closely than could traditional predators which were instinctively avoided. By the time that these grazing animals had developed an awareness of man-ape as predator our superior, structural fat-fed, brains had devised longer range killing apparatus which enabled him to hunt more effectively. Larger and more powerful man, more close in stature and power to the great apes, might have been able to scavenge; but tiny, less powerful man had to hunt to survive as a carnivore.

In Ardrey's thesis, our distant ancestor merely walked up on an unsuspecting, and heretofore unconditioned, grazing animals. By getting in so close, he could indeed slaughter a few of the beasts before the others scattered. Man undoubtedly used many tricks, such as the driving of animals over cliffs, surrounding them by fire, or trapping them in bogs. There the last, gasping efforts of the larger animals could be extinguished by even the most primitive weapons. Primitive man, hunting in social groups, may have attacked some larger animals in a way analogous to that used by packs of wild dogs. As one occupies the attention of the prey others rush in at the vulnerable spots, causing some damage, retreating, then attacking again opportunistically. But, unlike the dogs, man had weapons to use, and these were decisive.

Thus, man's earliest technological skills were employed in the fabrication of weaponry. In this confined sense, one might define man as, generally, a tool-making animal. Where some of the higher apes do use tools, they generally are wholly incapable of conceiving improvements to the basics found accidentally in nature. Man not only used weapons, he fabricated and slowly improved on their designs. Thus, he simply chipped away on rocks, not only to sharpen the cutting edges, but to create wholly new weapons unlike anything found naturally; or, if found accidentally in nature, to take other unshaped rocks and make them like unto that which was found to be most useful.

Of the discoveries listed among early man's possessions, all are apparently directly concerned with hunting and processing of the kill. Some tools were used in the actual hunt; others were used in skinning and cutting up the kill; and still others were used to grind up the bones to extract the marrow in the bones. Even man's early art was connected with the hunt.

In the famous Lascaux cave in France, and elsewhere scattered throughout the world, one finds evidence of man's prowess as a hunter. The subjects of these drawings, paintings, and carvings is nearly universal: man killing, or seeking to kill, his principal, perhaps favorite, prey. It has been suggested many times that the drawings may carry a quasi-religious significance, or may invoke a magic to aid in the hunt. Analogies have been drawn that suggest a number of very logical possibilities. For example, man may have sought to "capture" the animal in his drawings. Or he may have wished to learn more of its habits and its vulnerabilities by making pictures of it. He might even have tried a magic death wish in much the same way a witch-doctor might make a doll of an enemy and then jab pins through it. Indeed, this last suggestion is fully supported in many drawings wherein arrows or spears or merely stone knives are seen piercing the animals' bodies.

What we are then led to conclude is almost too simple. For the overwhelming bulk of man's existence on this earth his life has been wholly dominated by thoughts of the hunt. All that man did, thought, or worked at was vitally and necessarily related to the hunt. Unless man was successful in the hunt, he and his family, perhaps his clan or tribe, went without food, or without that which had become the staple of life. He might, in times of severe hunting failures, be able to survive on seasonally available vegetable matters, but this was at best a last ditch effort he would make at survival.

Conversely, a successful hunt, perhaps one in which he drove a herd of some especially succulent prey over a cliff, was the cause of great jubilation. It meant a time of plenty for the whole tribe. it meant great social status would accrue to the hunters. Thus, social status and perhaps overall leadership fell to the great hunters. In the entire chain of man's activities nothing was so clearly obvious to him than that success in hunting was noteworthy and praiseworthy. He had probably not yet learned to interrelate sexual intercourse with procreation. Indeed today some savages still have not made that inference. In Australia some of the aborigines still assume that the nearest large rock to a woman when she delivers a child is its father.

One can suggest two logical possibilities for the development of language that are related to hunting. In the one, man must learn to communicate in order to plan and execute the successful expedition. In the other, man learns to report his kill and, probably to brag about his successes. Both theories, and certainly the two taken together, are entirely plausible. If the thesis holds that man evolved all of his initial human skills around hunting, then it surely follows that his development of speech and communication can be related. The only other thesis that, in my opinion, bears any merit is that which relates speech to sexual encounters and to child-rearing. But, clearly, sexual encounters, especially of a primitive kind, do not require verbal communication. This is especially true of the animal kingdom beneath man. Other, instinctive signals suggest when such encounters are to be made. Later, as sex becomes in part an expression of love and recreation, not merely a seasonal impulse, then, perhaps, language became somewhat more important. But even this, one can relate to hunting. Man returned from the hunt to his mate and to the family, either because of instinct, or because he would receive sexual favors from the waiting female as a reward for being a good hunter and provider. It seems to me that any more permanent ties, those we hopefully recognize today as binding man to his family, must have come much, much later in man's history.

If man developed speech in order to better plan his hunts, this would fit well within the overall assumption that man became man in his hunting. Group hunting is certainly known in nature. Wild dogs hunt in packs; great cats often hunt in groups; and many other carnivores operate in groups. Recent observations of the animal kingdom have shown that animals ordinarily share their food only when the menu includes meat. Certain members of the monkey world do occasionally kill and eat meat. This is the only time they share their food. Thus, even in the animal kingdom it is generally only the meat-eating animals, or the herbivores which occasionally eat some meat, that share in a kind of social atmosphere.

Early man shared his meat, then, following an animal impulse. Thus, in the widest sense, carnivores may be expected to be "social" and the herbivores who occasionally eat meat may be expected to be "social" at that time. But the social activities of men are presumably of a higher and different order than the rest of the animal kingdom. They would become distinctively different—that is, human—if in the process of such social sharing, they added conversation, and even the most rudimentary communication. By the same token, connecting sexual favors to a successful hunt would uplift the social activity of hunting from a merely animal to a truly human activity. Nowhere in the animal kingdom would the female reward the male for a successful hunt by offering him sexual intercourse. If we extended this sexual reward idea a little more, to the point where the community gave successful hunters sexual rewards, e.g., by offering the most attractive female or a virgin, or the most accomplished lover, to the hunter, even the cause of natural selection and of desired procreation by the most desirable would be furthered. In any event, such ideas presume the human qualities of abstract thought, reward/punishment, and communication.

Even today we know that a successful hunt requires planning. This is true even in times that have produced the most sophisticated weapons in the form of high-powered (and thus long-range) rifles and telescopic sighting aids. It takes little to make the transition to the time when men would have had to cooperate. They were beings with no sophisticated weapons. They would have had to cooperate to the fullest. Since primitive man was among the slowest and weakest of the carnivores, he had to be able to use his one distinctive and wholly decisive power: his ability to think and to plan. All of that would have been dependent on communication, and, thus on speech.

One can easily envision primitive men planning how to drive an elephant into a mire, or a giant pig into a bog, or a herd of cows over a cliff. We can see in the mind's eye how important it might be that each be in his proper position and that each do his assigned task. We can see how the success of the hunt depended on timing and reasonably precision teamwork. We can also understand that man had to know and communicate about one of those beneficial accidents of nature, such as a lightning-induced forest fire. Then all hunters would assemble to use this fire to their benefit. And, certainly not least, one can see the need to communicate the accumulation of wisdom of past experience in hunting to the new generation of hunters. Failure to communicate such skills would jeopardize the existence of the entire group.

Finally, one can see how this communication of knowledge could easily be telescoped into a session of bragging about one's past successes. One could communicate how the buffalo was killed, while at the same time adding to his legend as a great hunter. As man mastered fire, one can surely see the primitive equivalent of a contemporary hunter's campfire, around which each member of the hunting party vies to outdo his peers in bragging of his greatest accomplishments as a hunter. Again, such comradeship is unthinkable without some form of speech communication.

The base line of the argument is this: that modern man's social organization and his speech communication had its most probable origins in hunting. For the overwhelming bulk of man's time on earth, nearly all things, from communication to art, had their roots in hunting. Man's myths and his religion were vitally interconnected with hunting. If we remove hunting from man's history we create only a giant void that cannot otherwise be filled, and we surely lead to a misunderstanding of man.

Man's unique method of hunting may also be said to be responsible for man's social relations. One of the major conclusions animal behavior scientists have drawn from meat-eating animals in general is that the hunt and the consequent meal are shared activities. While animals do not share meals based on nuts, fruits and vegetables, they do share meals based on the killing of other animals. Those species which are omnivorous share within the group only when they are eating meat. There is no evidence that either herbivores or omnivores ever share plant-based meals.

If man truly shares in the general rules of behavior within the animal kingdom then he had to become at least an omnivore to become social in the most fundamentally demanded behavior of all species, eating. All of the existing anthropological evidence points to man as a communal carnivore in even his earliest human behavior.

With man's capacity for both abstract thought and speech, the meal provided by the hunt offered a truly splendid opportunity to become social. There is every logical reason to assume that man talked about the past hunting successes, grumbled about the hunt's failures, and planned the next day's hunt. As he spun his tale, fanciful elements would have been introduced. Primitive man could have easily introduced elements into the conversations, elements that might later have formed the basis of religion and myths.

The meals would have provided an excellent opportunity to choose leaders and to establish various forms of rank within the group. The great hunter would logically have been honored at such feasts, and the unsuccessful hunter might, with equal logic, be demoted or disgraced. Certainly, the criteria for promotion and demotion would be clear in a society so tied to the hunt as its single, supreme necessity.

There is also considerable evidence that primitive man thought of the hunt as the most logical subject of his art. In addition to the probable magic content of the cave paintings and rock drawings that early man fabricated with probable reference to success in the hunt, he also exhibited his purely aesthetic powers in the creation of weaponry more beautiful than would ever be needed merely for practical purposes. Some of the many truly beautiful knives and spearheads may have been badges of authority or magical instruments, but they are also quite enviable works of art in and of themselves.

The most deadly of man's impulses is to war against his fellows.[6] Destruction of other members of the same species is something almost confined to man alone. Some male members of lower species do, of course, engage rather regularly in war-like activities, primarily to establish pecking orders and to establish territorial claims. In many species that are harem-oriented the male with the control over the females must stand challenges from other males at a time roughly coinciding with mating season. Scientists have observed that it is of the highest importance in some animal species to establish dominance in some male. When this cannot be established easily a fight may occur, but only rarely are these battles fatal to any of the participants. Once dominance is established all returns to normal.

Many species are quite territorial. Much has been written on this subject in books such as Robert Ardery's *The Territorial Imperative* (1966). Birds and mammals, reptiles and amphibians of many species try to control a specific area, allowing no others of their species to invade. Occasionally, some species may try to keep other whole species out of their established territory. In the process of defending their territories some animals behave as though they were making war.

Innate in some species is a kind of cannibalism. Some females, especially in the insect world, may occasionally eat their recent mates. Some fathers or mothers may attempt to eat their offspring, and in some cases the young may attempt to eat one another until only a few survive. We are treading very familiar ground here and have added nothing new. There is only one question which interests us: Is man's cannibal and warlike behavior merely a form of instinct left over from his animal heritage, or is it tied to man's behavior toward his fellow man; that is, is war a social activity?

There will never be a clearcut answer to our fundamental question. Some of man's aggression may have been left over from his animal ancestry in the form of unreasoned instincts. We are learning now that some animals, even of the higher primate class, do kill others of their species for no apparent reason, engaging even at times in cannibalism. But we have also yet to establish that animals commit aggression without a compelling reason, e.g., such as being driven out of their natural habitat by some change in climate and/or surroundings. The idea of mere territorial aggrandizement seems to fall exclusively into human habits.

Perhaps some of our primitive ancestors, similar to the aborigine of today, engaged in cannibalism for ritualistic reasons. Perhaps they sought to capture another warrior's virtue by eating his flesh. And, perhaps, they had failed to be successful in their hunting and sought merely to survive. Perhaps, as well, they saw no unity in humankind, and then saw nothing especially wrong in hunting and killing others in different tribes. Many primitives make no distinction between man and the animals, so it may be that they see nothing wrong in eating other humans since these other humans are merely another form of life to be taken for survival.

Human wars are a different matter. For my purposes here I shall refer to wars to gain territory, possessions, and prisoners as "human wars."

There is nothing to correspond to these types of activities among the animal species. Human beings have, as long as we can tell, made war on one another. Archaeologists have uncovered the bones of many early men (perhaps, pre-men, in some cases) who have been purposely killed. Of course, we can never establish when the first war of aggression took place; nor can we ever say for certain that such and such a pre-man or early man was definitely killed for a specific purpose. It seems rather clear that many pre-men and early men were killed and eaten by others of a similar type. We find their bones scraped and crushed, proving that a tool-using being ate of their flesh.

Alexander the Great was shocked to learn that it was the custom of certain Eastern tribes against whom he fought to eat the dead. Those who died a hero's death were especially coveted, presumably because that flesh could convey certain heroic characteristics to the eater. It is possible that early primitive man did not practice cannibalism except on his own dead. There is nothing within the findings we have discussed that would preclude that conclusion. It is at least possible that cannibalism was begun only after the practice of eating the fallen of a tribe had been established. Having shown that human flesh was desirable the community may have sought out its victims in times when there were no dead heroes to eat.

There is much evidence available today that might lead one to the conclusion that the first great war was between our direct ancestors, those commonly called Cro-Magnon men, and the Neanderthals. Cro-Magnon men probably came from the East and met the stronger, but less gifted Neanderthals. All of the archaeological evidence shows that the period of coexistence was, at best, extremely brief. Our ancestors coveted the land, hunting ranges, and lodgings of the Neanderthals. Thus, they killed off the Neanderthals and took their properties. One can speculate that such killings might easily have taken place over two million or more years, as a superior group of early or pre-men found less gifted and able rivals and destroyed them. This is surely one way we can account for the disappearance of many early human or slightly subhuman species.

Against this background, we are not speculating much more when we suggest that war originated in rivalries for hunting grounds. Much later, of course, at and before the dawn of recorded history, men fought over arable land, as men emerged at the hunting and gathering and tilling stage of human existence. As wars became more complex, demanding more and more skills and resources, men organized in increasingly complex ways. As game became scarce, as men killed off whole species of game which were easily killed, rivalries for hunting grounds must have increased.

As political systems were organized, and as game continued to remain scarce, the few, remaining hunting areas became royal preserves. Only the privileged few were permitted to hunt. For the rest, all that remained were the few domesticated animals and the land with its crops. At this point hunting ceased to be a standard way of life, but we can certainly envision kings taking nations to war to obtain new hunting grounds for their personal pleasure.

While hunting was all but abandoned as a standard method of existence, there remained within man that deep instinctive voice, a voice which even today impels him toward hunting. That voice is over two million years old. It is most unlikely that it will die out soon.

Our conclusions in this section are quite simple and very logical. Primitive man was a hunter, not a scavenger. Surely, if he could not kill game animals of several sizes, from the tiniest to the largest, he could not be expected to have been able to kill or drive off the stronger predators in each size class.

Second, we have seen that there is, presently, great evidence to suggest that without meat man might have remained an underdeveloped ape. The fatty acids that only meat can provide, and which cannot be provided in any way by plant food, are apparently wholly necessary not only to brain growth, but most importantly, to brain development and ordering.

Third, we have concluded that man developed a human way of hunting. He was not truly descended from predator-carnivores, and thus had to develop unique ways of hunting within general limitations of animals. Since he was not equipped specifically to kill other animals in order to survive, man had to hunt in a human way, that is, with tools and weapons.

Man would not be man in an historical sense if we were to strip him of his vital connection to his weapons. While some apes might on rare occasion use tools, they do not do so generally. While some apes may eat meat occasionally, they do not eat meat as their standard diet. In general, they could not become carnivores because they are not well equipped for the hunting life, and they could not—or at least did not—come to the use of tools and weapons as standard and usual extensions of themselves. One can then state the premise either way with equal certitude: man is man because he uses tools regularly and essentially; and man can use tools because he has attributes, namely the use of tools, that set him high above his cousins in the animal world.

Had the apes used tools, had they chosen to live a more rigorous life in the plains and valleys, and not in the relative security of the jungle, they might have created challenges for themselves to which they would have responded adequately (i.e., by learning to hunt), or to which they would have been unequal and thus would have vanished.

Man alone chose to become a predator without the adequate physical equipment to do so; and he responded by compensating—by developing and using weapons. Perhaps many individuials and many clans were unable to respond to the environment's challenge and perished; the point is that a sufficient number survived to provide a human population for the world.

One may argue with those who hold hunting in low esteem that it is most natural for man to be hunter and least natural for him to oppose it. If we are to ascend to new heights, moving above the animal instinct for the hunt, let us at least acknowledge that man has been a hunter for all but a very few moments of his multimillion year existence, and that change comes but slowly in ways so long a habit. But when we move away from hunting let us not forget that our species has evolved in such a way as to be dependent on animal tissue for at least those vital complex fatty acids found only in meat. We have synthesized many chemicals that are absolutely vital to man; perhaps, these fatty acids can also be fabricated. But we may one day discover other meat derivatives man has also come to depend on. Then we will duplicate unnaturally again the vital nutrients that man has, traditionally and naturally, taken from meats. The opponents of hunting would not, themselves, be here and present today, existing in their present mode, were it not for the hunters in their past.

Hunting in the Judaeo-Christian Tradition

By the time we meet the Jews of the Old Testament they are already settled into an agricultural way of life. They are no longer hunters or mere gatherers of what nature has provided; they are civilized city-dwellers who plant and harvest. They raise sheep and goats and cattle. There is no special interest in hunting. Few of the Hebrews we are exposed to in the Biblical writings kill wild animals save to protect themselves and their domesticated herds.

The Hebrew Language of the Old Testament is rich in hunting vocabulary. The word *tsud*[1] or *tsadah*[2] means to hunt or to lie in wait, as for wild animals. *Radaph*[3] means to pursue or to chase in the process of hunting game. *Tasyid*[4] means to capture, in the sense of fulfillment of the successful hunt. In Ezekiel we find the term *metsudah*[5] relating to the hunt, in the sense of an object for hunting, or the hunted. The Jews may not have hunted in Biblical times, but their language suggests that there was a time when men regularly hunted.

In the original Hebrew *harag* meant to kill an inferior being such as an animal, although the word is used occasionally to convey the idea of taking human life. Here it is probably used metaphorically. The normal words for killing a man were *muth,* to put to death, and *nakah,* to smite, and *gatal,* to kill. A different word, *sabach* (also: *tabach* and *shachat*) was used to slaughter domesticated animals.[6]

The Jewish recollection of hunting is dim in the Bible. Adam and Cain are described as farmers; Abel is a shepherd. Isaac and Jacob are contrasted with the hunting tribal leaders, for they are no longer hunters. But the term *kethibh* (hunting)[7] in Genesis suggests that at one time food (*zedah*) was obtained in this way.

The people of Israel knew something of hunting, as in the stories of eating hart (Deut., 12:15-22) and roebuck (1 Kings 13, 24), and venison (Gen. 27). The Jews used traditional hunting weapons including slings (1 Sam. 17:40), nets (Job 18:6; Ps. 9:15; Isa. 15:20; Ps. 35:7), snares and traps (Amos 3:5; Eccles. 9:12; Job 18:8-10); bows and arrows (Gen. 27:3) and pits (Isa. 24:17; Ps. 35, 7). In the Apocrypha, hunters decoy partridges (Sir. 11:30), snare gazelles (Sir. 27:20) and eat game as a regular part of the diet (Sir. 36:19).

33

According to Josephus, Herod the Great was a mighty hunter and used dogs as a normal part of his hunting.

Deuteronomy (espec. 14) shows that there was some game in the countryside, although the characters introduced there are not shown as hunters. One primary purpose of this book of the Bible was to differentiate between "clean" and "unclean" animals, that is, those which the faithful could eat and those which they were forbidden to eat. The dichotomy was made not on how the animals were taken, that is, whether they were killed in the hunt or whether they were domesticated animals slaughtered, but, rather, according to the nature of the animal.

Hunting was not condemned anywhere in the Old Testament. Indeed, Nimrod, founder of Assyria, is credited with having been "a mighty hunter before Jehovah."

Ishmael the Archer and Esau the "cunning hunter" are praiseworthy characters. Isaac is reported to have loved his son Esau because of the latter's success at hunting: "and Isaac loved Esau because he did eat of his venison. . . ." The unfortunate Esau apparently returned from a hunt empty-handed, and his brother Jacob refused to feed him until Esau sold him his birthright. After protesting that this was not right, Esau gave in. He was despised for having sold out so cheaply; but he was not condemned for having been a hunter (see 27, 30). After Esau had been cursed for denying his birthright his father Isaac called him to his deathbed, asking him to bring him once more some venison from the hunt. Isaac was dying and unable to distinguish between goat meat and venison, and Jacob deceived his father by bringing the meat of two kids. It is clear that Isaac viewed venison as a delicacy, whereas the meat of domesticated animals was commonplace; as Isaac recognized, it would have been far easier to have ordered the kids slaughtered. When Jacob brought the goat meat, Isaac expressed surprise that the venison had been obtained so quickly. In his blessing Isaac noted that the smell of the goat skins that Jacob used to make him appear like Esau was good. Isaac confused that odor with the smell of the hunter and said ". . . the smell of my son is the smell of a field which the Lord hath blessed."

In Leviticus (17:13) the Hebrews are instructed to bleed any kill made in the hunt because they are forbidden to eat the blood. But beyond the proscription against eating the blood there is nothing said to prohibit hunting; indeed, it seems to be a wholly acceptable way of obtaining fresh meat. This same proscription applies to domesticated animals. Later (Lev. 17:15), it is proscribed to eat an animal which has died of natural causes, or which has been killed by other predators. In short, man is not permitted to scavenge, although he may hunt and kill animals of the forest himself.

In the Book of Proverbs (12:27) man is admonished not to waste what he has taken in the hunt. The sin of sloth is described using the example of one who hunts but does not cook (or, presumably, eat) what he has killed. The diligent person would kill and not waste the product of his successful hunt.

During the Exodus the Lord provided the people of Israel with a foodstuff called manna, but the people wanted meat as well. The Lord promised "At even(ing) ye shall eat flesh. . . ." God then caused quail to appear in vast numbers, and the people ate of these, having snared them in nets and clubbed them to death (Exod. 16:13ff).

The vast majority of the hunters were Gentiles. The Hebrews had left the hunting life and had become settled, or, as in the Exodus, were searching for land to settle and to till. Among the non-Jews, Nimrod is especially noteworthy because of the praise lavished on him by the writer of Genesis. Nimrod ". . . began to be a mighty one in the earth. He was a mighty hunter before the Lord; wherefore it is said, Even as Nimrod, the mighty hunter before the Lord" (Gen. 10:8-9).

The only negative suggestion that can be made concerning hunting in the Old Testament concerns the nature of Cain's punishment for slaying Abel. The Lord told Cain that he could not become a farmer, for, "when thou tillest the ground, it shall henceforth not yield unto thee her strength; and a vagabond shalt thou be in the earth" (Gen. 4-12). A reasonable reading of the passage suggests that Cain was condemned to be a hunter, a person who could not earn his daily bread by tilling the fields. But a fair reading also suggests that the punishment consists in not having roots, not in being forced to hunt. That is, Cain was denied a place of his own, condemned to be a wanderer, and thus had to hunt; he was not made a hunter as a punishment. There was no onus attached to hunting. One could hunt whether he had a permanent residence and cultivated fields or not. But he who had no permanent residence, who had no crops in his fields, was condemned to being a hunter and gatherer. As only a hunter, Cain could not become "civilized," as was the case with his younger brothers who were born after

Abel's death, those who founded the cities noted in the remainder of Genesis 10.

Among those who killed wild beasts in the Old Testament were David and Samson. In Judges (14:5-6) Samson killed a lion: ". . . and, behold, a young lion roared against him and the Spirit of the Lord came mightily upon him and he rent him as he would have rent a kid. . . ." In David's case he was confronted with both a lion and a bear, "And thy servant slew both the lion and the bear. . . ." (1 Sam. 17:36). In Second Samuel we read of Benaiah's slaying of a lion: "And Benaiah, the son of Jehoiada, the son of a valiant man, of Kabzeel, who had done many acts . . . he went down also and slew a lion in the midst of a pit in time of snow (2 Sam. 23:20). In this case it is not clear that Benaiah was being threatened or that any of his property was in jeopardy; it is possible that he killed the lion for sport or pleasure, or to establish his reputation as a hunter.

Perhaps it is because the Hebrews were not ordinarily hunters that it is noteworthy that such figures as Benaiah had hunted and killed dangerous prey. That venison was a delicacy suggests that it was not a common dish on the tables of the Old Testament figures. If the killing of wild animals for protection, sport, or meat was ordinary it would not merit recognition when it was done. In the case of Benaiah it seems that only two things distinguish him: that he killed the lion in the pit, and that he slew two formidable enemies, described as "lionlike."

In general, the theology of the ancient people of Israel recognized the substantial difference between man and animals. Early on, God, having created all sorts of animals and birds and fishes, gave man complete control over all that God had created. "So God created man in his own image, in the image of God he created him; male and female he created them. And God blessed them, and God said unto them, Be fruitful and multiply and replenish the earth and subdue it; and have dominion over the fish of the sea, and over the fowl of the air, and every other living thing that moveth upon the earth" (Gen. 1:27-28).

It is possible to interpret Genesis (especially 1:29-30) to conclude that originally man and all the animals were vegetarians. God gives "seed-bearing plants" and "all green plants" to both man and all animal life for food. It is not clear when this was changed, but presumably it was altered by the time of the fall of Adam from God's grace. From what we know of animal, fish, and bird life, there was never a time when only herbivores existed. The language of Genesis 1:29-30 suggests more than life ("whatsoever breatheth") could eat of vegetables and other things than that sentient life was limited exclusively to seeds and plants. The passage does not condemn the eating of flesh. It is compelling that we conclude that, whatever the condition in the Garden of Eden, by the time historical man appears, it is permissible to eat plants and flesh. This is precisely the point made in Deuteronomy: how and under what conditions which kinds of animals may be killed and their flesh incorporated in the human diet.

Old Testament religion is quite clear on the doctrine of sin. One may commit sin against one's fellow man, that is, creatures of the same order of creation; and one can commit sin against the higher power, namely, against Jehovah. The latter case is very clear, for the very first instance of sin (Gen. 3) occurred as disobedience of God's orders concerning the eating of the fruit of the tree of the knowledge of good and evil. It may be argued that, without God, sin would be impossible, even against one's fellow man. That is, we can sin against our neighbor only because God has made it a sin, by requiring a code of interpersonal conduct among men. Animals are considered only insofar as they are the possessions of men, or when the treatment of animals might have a bearing on relations among men, or between man and God.

In Exodus 21 the author codified the law concerning man's treatment of certain domesticated animals, notably the ox. Essentially, this law creates the conditions under which the owner of oxen is injured when another human being causes harm to his possessions. The sin is not associated with the animal directly. It is fair to conclude that, according to the Old Testament, man cannot sin against an animal. Man is related to the animals as their superior, since he has been given full dominion over them.

In one common conception, not to love God or one's fellow man is the essential content of sin. Thus, in killing another's domesticated animal or pet, man has sinned against his neighbor by denying love to that person. In killing more game in the hunt than one can use, one might sin against others who might wish to hunt, but only if that overkill added to the scarcity of game, causing hardship to the neighbor.

We have already accepted the point of view that man may hunt with great anticipation of the kill. He may savor the kill, deriving pleasure from the taking of animal life. We have also established that anthropological man, from the very beginnings of our non-

Biblical study of him, was a brute hunter, killing with cold-blooded aggressiveness. Even from earliest times, man the hunter may have approached the hunt more from the perspective of the pleasure the hunt gave than from that of merely obtaining meat for the family or the clan. He may have been infinitely more interested in gaining the social acceptance resulting from being a great and respected hunter than in acquiring basic foodstuff. None of this is even remotely suggestive of sin, unless it becomes false or over-whelming pride. That is, man may become too prideful and thus harm his own character, or he may do harm to others in the expression of his over-powering pride. But this is not the necessary consequence of the hunt; it is the possible, not necessary or probable, result of success in hunting. It represents a flaw in character, not a flaw in action.

The analogy is clear between false pride in hunting and false pride and egoism in any other human activity. One can misbehave in anything that is human. Man may romantically engage in false pride; he may show egoism in the manipulation of other men; and he may become prideful in politics. Such sin is not inherent in any of these activities; rather, it is the consequence of the lack of love and charity in interpersonal relations.

The New Testament says absolutely nothing about hunting. However, it says a great deal about fishing. The best we can do is to fabricate an argument on the analogy between the taking of the life of a fish, also a living and breathing and sentient being, and the taking of animal or bird life.

Christ took bread and two fishes, "and looking up to heaven, he blessed, and brake . . . and they did all eat, and were filled" (Matt. 14:19-20). And, again, "he took seven loaves and the fishes, and gave thanks . . . and gave to his disciples, and the disciples to the multitude" (Matt. 15:36-37). In Mark (6:38-44), Christ ". . . the two fishes divided he among them all." The same command to eat of the fish available was recorded in Mark 8:7-8. Luke reports the same distributions of fish among those who listened to Jesus (Luke 9:13-16) as does John (6:11-12).

Christ ate fish on at least one instance, this being after the Resurrection. "And when he had thus spoken, he shewed them his hands and his feet. . . . He said unto them, have ye here any meat? And they gave him a piece of a broiled fish . . . and he took it and did eat before them" (Luke 24:41-43). One may suggest that Christ asked for meat without stipulating whether it was to be of fish, fowl, or animal. Since it was traditional to slaughter a lamb at Passover, it is probable that Christ, during most of his years on earth, ate of that meat, at least once a year. Clearly, there is no proscription in the New Testament against eating fish or meat.

Christ ordered his disciples to fish on at least two occasions. Several of the twelve disciples were fishermen by profession (Mark 1:16-17; Matt. 4:18-19), and the New Testament records no onus being attached to that profession. When a profession was held in contempt, as was the case with Judas, a tax collector, this was noted. Although Jesus took the fishermen away from fishing, making them "fishers of men," they did occasionally return to their old profession. Jesus came to his disciples, at the Sea of Tiberius, apparently after some period of absence. "Then Jesus saith unto them, Children, have ye any meat? They answered him, No. And he said unto them, cast the net on the right side of the ship, and ye shall find. They cast therefore, and now they were not able to draw it for the multitude of fishes" (John 21; Luke 5). The second instance of Christ ordering his disciples to fish occurs in Matthew (17:27): ". . . Go thou to the sea, and cast an hook, and take up the fish that first cometh up. . . ."

The passage which is most often quoted as showing that Christ disapproved of hunting or the killing of animals, that "not one of these [sparrows] will fall to the ground without your Father's will" (Matt. 10:29) is misused here, for it applies not to hunting, but to God's providential sovereignty over all things.

In the Book of Mormon one finds many favorable references to hunting. Apparently, the profession of hunter was held in high esteem by the peoples described therein. "And it came to pass that Lib also did that which was good in the sight of the Lord. . . . And Lib also himself became a great hunter" (Ether 10:19). Also, Nephi, author of three books within the Book of Mormon, says of himself, . . . I did slay wild beasts, insomuch that I did obtain food for our families" (1 Nephi 16:32). In a wilderness Nephi found ". . . the wild goat and all manner of wild animals, which were for the use of men" (2 Nephi 2:15). Enos also hunted: "Behold, I went to hunt wild beasts in the forests. . . ." (Enos 1:3).

The peoples of the Book of Mormon apparently faced an almost overwhelming challenge from wild beasts. It is related in several places (Jaron 1:6; Mosiah 18:4; Alma 2:37) that a wilderness existed wherein man could scarcely compete with the ferocious animals that lived there. Here, hunting would be done for self-preservation.

The scarcity of game, so well known in the Old World, was not a problem for the peoples of the Western Hemisphere. Just as the colonists discovered when they began to settle here in the 16th century, game was abundant nearly everywhere and one could nearly always provide food by hunting. Still, the people set aside wilderness areas as wildlife refuges and hunting grounds so that an abundance of game and a recreational area for hunting would always be available. "And they built a great city . . . and they did preserve the land southward for a wilderness, to get game [although] . . . the whole face of the land northward was covered with inhabitants" (Ether 10:20-21).

One who wishes to condemn hunting as immoral must look to authorities other than traditional religious works for support. The entire Judaeo-Christian synthesis suggests that it is quite correct for man to hunt if he wishes to do so. There is not a single passage that condemns hunting or hunters. Nowhere in the Bible, nor in the Book of Mormon, can one find anything negative attached to the act of hunting or to the profession or the sport of the hunter.

The only rules that are attached to hunting are those that are the general Christian principles that can be, and necessarily are, applied to all human acativities. One may not negate the obligation of love and charity in pursuing any human action. One may not act in a way that brings harm or injury to his neighbor, disgrace upon himself, or which interferes with his love of God. If hunting passes these tests, that is, if it is regulated human conduct which is made obedient to accepted ethical standards, then it is permitted.

Of course, one is certainly not compelled to hunt; nor is one required to eat meat from any source. It is a voluntary action. Man may himself kill meat (hunting), or he may have it killed for him (slaughtering). These actions are permissive; but they are not prohibited.[8]

Our Hunting Heritage: Europe

It is probable that as man entered organized society and created the state mechanism he began to control hunting rights. Many of man's earliest wars were fought over hunting rights. Likewise, political leaders established hunting privileges for themselves and their friends and court favorites. Slaves certainly would never have been granted hunting rights. The semi-free serfs and tillers of the land would have been locked in place on the land and deprived of hunting rights.

Pharoh Tuthmoses (c.1400 B.C.) is said to have killed 120 elephants at water holes in one year. It is probable that he impressed peasants to serve in his hunts. Around 850 B.C. the Assyrian King Ashurnasipal II gave an account of one hunt on which he killed 450 lions, 390 wild bulls, 200 ostriches and 30 elephants. Again, it is highly likely that he used his soldiers, peasants and slaves to corral the game.[1]

History records that the nobility of all ancient kingdoms liked to hunt. Since game is known to have been scarce we can assume that laws were made restricting hunting to the privileged classes. These might be properly called a warrior-hunter elite. Hunting skills were clearly believed to sharpen military skills. Hunting rights also served as a form of reward for valor in battle.

The first extant laws on hunting are Roman. Certain parks were set aside by law early in Roman history as game preserves of the rich. Many early Roman military leaders were granted hunting privileges for service to the expanding Republic. The Romans also restricted hunting in areas under cultivation. Roman treatises[2] on hunting tell us why this was done. The Romans hunted with hounds and horses, and thus a hunt could ruin the farms and endanger the farmers.

The Romans regarded only certain species of game as worthy of the organized hunt of the warrior-hunter. Thus, peasants were ordinarily permitted to hunt small game such as hares, hedgehogs, rabbits, and the like. Conversely, only the aristocrats could hunt the stag, fox, wolf, and bear. Later, of course, more exotic species, especially those native to Africa and Asia were hunted only by warrior-aristocrats.

Hunting with falcons and other trained birds of prey was again restricted in antiquity to the nobility. Certain breeds of dogs, such as the greyhound, were reserved by law to the nobility. The Egyptian pharohs and the Roman generals shared such exclusive rights. Conversely, mixed breeds were kept by the commoners who used them to hunt small animals.

Roman hunting and agricultural practices had depleted much of the readily available European and African game in areas under their control long before the Empire fell. Cultivation of single crops in many areas turned once fertile land into desert. Changes of irrigation practices wiped out natural water holes. The taking of game for the Colosseum depleted once plentiful herds as well. Game was almost nonexistent along the African coastline and in accessible areas of Italy and France and Spain. Consequently, highly restrictive laws were promulgated, limiting hunting even among the nobility. Most of these laws were ignored, excepting, of course, their enforcement against the poor. It was a classic case of too little control coming far too late. Also, there was no real knowledge of the science of game management.

As Roman areas were overrun by barbarians, the remaining game was all but wiped out by peasants seeking food, and by armies seeking to sustain themselves. Once again, those with the military and political power sought to limit the hunting of those who had no power or might. Whole areas were depleted of game of all sizes and kinds.

Waves of migrating barbarians moved across Germany and succeeded in rendering extinct many species of animals that had been common through the time that Caesar had fought the Germanic tribes. In his *Commentaries on the Gallic Wars,* Caesar noted that wolves, bear, stags, bison, auroch, and elk were common in Germany. He also noted a great egalitarianism among the Germans in hunting all species of game. It was still so abundant that no controls had yet been established over the hunt. From noble to commoner, all hunted only when needed for food or clothing. But the vast migrations of peoples over the next few centuries destroyed the great herds and destroyed whole species in many areas. Class-oriented game laws were laid down by the kings and nobles.

Early in British history we find a series of game laws issued by various kings. In one of the first King Edgar (959-79) imposed an annual tax on the Welsh of 300 wolf skins per year. This tax was imposed primarily to destroy these predators and thus allow more game to live only to be hunted by the nobility. There is no clear record that the tax was paid at any time or how long the law lasted or whether it did have the desired effect of reducing the wolf population.[3]

The oldest extant English law dates to the Danish King, Cnute (1016-35) and was promulgated in 1016. It reads in part: "I will that each one shall be worthy of such venerie as he, by hunting, can take, either in the plains or in the woods within his own fee or dominion, but each shall abstain from my venerie in every place where I will that my beasts shall have firm peace and quietude. . . ." The King clearly had set aside an area for his own use. The penalty for hunting on the King's Land was severe in Cnute's time: death or disfigurement. The law also makes it clear that a grant of land brought with it all that existed on that land, including game. It might be more precise to say that the right to hunt was included in property land grants issued by kings in the eleventh century, and probably before. The landowner was free to use his hunting rights as he chose, as with other land-based property rights, so long as the king continued his land grant.

English common law from the beginnings noted that animals were of two types: domestic and wild. Those that were considered wild existed *ferrus naturae*. They could not be owned, in and of themselves. However, one could own the right to hunt these animals. This was the claim made by generations of kings in the king's dominion and by nobles on their own lands. If land changed hands, always with or by the king's consent, the hunting rights accruing to the land went part and parcel with the land.

English common law implicitly recognized game management and conservation. The continued scarcity of game mitigated against universal hunting rights. These rights to hunt were invested in the warrior-nobility class. They could stock the castle larder by hunting on their own property at will, or they could hunt on other land by invitation. They could share or not share with the peasants as they chose, for they were, for all intents and purposes, their own law in regard to the peasantry-serf class.

The common law also recognized an obligation on the peasant-serf class to assist the nobility in hunting. This was, of course, only one small part of their terrible burden of obligations to the lord of the manor. They were required to serve as beaters, chasing the game out of the forest retreats so that the lords could slaughter them. There certain risks evolved, and eventually the law came to recognize at least minimal obligations of the nobility to provide for some support of those who were injured, and for the families of those killed in the hunt.

After the Norman invasion of 1066 several changes were wrought in the English game laws. More severe limitations were placed on hunting, primarily as a means of enforcing obedience to the Norman rule. Hunting was accomplished more commonly with dogs than with serfs. Peasants were used mostly as trackers and game wardens, rather than as beaters. To their credit, the Normans also introduced the practice of announcing various stages of the hunt by the sounding of the horn. This gave some warning to the serfs as to the whereabouts of the hunters and what might be expected of their behavior when they appeared. Incidentally, the Norman practice of noting the sighting of a stag by calling out, "Thiaulau" gave rise to the cry of "Tally-ho!" in the fox hunt.

The Normans also introduced the hare to England. Although known in Europe even before Roman times, it had never been bred in England. This became a staple in the commoner's diet, and it was generally allowed to him as an animal he might hunt without arousing the ire of the nobility. The hare multiplied rapidly and was never endangered as a species by hunters.

William the Conquerer (1066-87) and his successors ruthlessly enforced the hunting laws against commoners who sought to hunt major species. William's law read,[4] "Whoever shall kill a stag, a wild boar, or even a hare, shall have his eyes torn out." The proscription against hunting hares was, as we saw, relaxed after they became plentiful. William bought allies, especially among the clerics, by granting hunting privileges. Soon after he had won at Hastings he appeased certain church dignitaries by granting hunting warrants. One such grant given to the Abbot of Battle Abbey still survives.

As a means of enforcing compliance with his new government, William developed the concept of "afforesting" large land areas. The king thus claimed title not to the land itself, but to certain land rights. These claims extended to gathering firewood and hunting and, in some cases, to grazing. He started a whole new bureaucracy that controlled the king's afforested areas. He claimed revenues from the sale of wood and game even to those who otherwise held title to that land.

William's successors were quick to recognize the potential of restrictive laws on the forests. With that powerful weapon in hand they soon made the forest laws most oppressive. One period commentator said of William Rufus (1087-1166) the king who followed the Conquerer, that he had made the forest laws "burdensome to baron and villain alike." The see-saw of power continued for centuries between the king and the nobility over control of the afforestations established by William I.

The Assize of the Forest is the first major official act of legislation dealing wholly with the forest and its animal inhabitants.[5] Promulgated by Henry II (1154-89) in 1184, it is sometimes called the Assize of Woodstock for it is known that he formulated legislation there at a council in the same year. Article XII is known to have been created at Woodstock, although other parts are presumed to have been mere restatements of earlier laws dealing with the subject. There is no evidence of the size of Henry's forests, although they are presumed to have been large.

The assize and subsequent action by the immediate successors of Henry II created a whole administrative hierarchy to deal with the king's pleasure in the forests that the crown claimed. This hierarchy included forest justices, game wardens, master woodsmen and others. Administrative officers whose whole concern was the forest may have existed prior to 1184, but the Assize of the Forest clearly established the legal bases for these offices. Their duties and offices were to continue in an almost unbroken line to the present.

The king recognized that he could not own game animals of the forest. However, he clearly could speak of the property rights of the right to hunt such wildlife. Here is a clear recognition that animals exist *ferrae naturae* free in nature. There is thus a qualitative difference between wild animals and domesticated animals. Domesticated animals had long been protected under laws promulgated by the predecessors to Henry II. Individuals can own, as the king's law permitted, animals which had been domesticated. This claim to domestication extended only to such species as the king chose to recognize, and not to individual animals which, although otherwise wild, had been raised and perhaps trained in captivity.

The Assize of the Forest was primarily concerned with deer hunting. Other wild animals suitable to capture or kill may have been included by inference. However, only deer were named by species.

Henry II regarded hunting rights as a form of property rights. In article II he states that "he forbids that anyone shall transgress against him in regard to his hunting rights or his forests in any respect. . . ."[6] These were regarded as a separate area of rights only incidentally related to to other rights of the woods. "He graciously allows them [the commoners] to take from the woods what they need" in firewood or lumber provided "this is done without wasting, and at the oversight of the king's forester."[7] No similar provision was made for harvesting game by commoners. The law merely provides that no one "shall transgress either in regard to his venison or his forests"[8] and that such transgressors, if caught by the foresters, shall be liable to punishment or fine. Indeed, those to whom the right to hunt in the king's forest is proscribed include "archbishops, bishops, earls, barons, knights, freeholders and all men."[9]

The king ordered that twelve knights be appointed to look out for his hunting rights. This visitation was a regular part of the administration of the forest and technically was carried out every three years. In reality these knights were charged with constant supervision. They were to make certain that the slaughter of animals in the king's woods was not being carried out. The king had forests in a number of counties and the responsibility of the knights extended to "any county in which he has venison."[10]

There was a conservationist aspect to the establishment of the king's forests in the various well-wooded counties of England. As a period dialogue noted, "The king's forest is a safe refuge for wild beasts; not every kind of beast, but those that live in the woods." Woods not belonging to the king himself could be appropriated to serve as animal refuge. There were royal forests established "where there are hiding places and rich pasture for wild beasts. Nor does it matter to whom the woods belong. . . ."[11]

No doubt one of the king's greatest concerns was the establishment of a royal hunting grounds, located so that well-stocked land would be readily available wherever the king happened to be. The kings of England, as elsewhere in the world, enjoyed hunting. Since the king's forests were posted to the common man, indeed, to any but those chosen by the king, the lands were plentifully stocked with all sorts of animals, ensuring a good hunt when it was the pleasure of the king to hunt. Further, the king's table would always be guaranteed a goodly supply of wildlife for banquets.

Although many offices had been created with special concern for the forest and the protection of animals the English sheriff was intermittently involved with such law enforcement. The sheriff had broad powers and duties. Many sheriffs clearly overstepped the legal boundries of the office in the enforcement of laws. Under Edward the Confessor (1042-66) the sheriff was ordinarily a small landowner, and the office was subordinate to earls. After 1170 the office grew in importance and the sheriffs became major law enforcement officers. Frequently, the sheriffs policed the woodlands, whether royal or otherwise. Many made and enforced rules in the forests and controlled hunting there. Their power was most frequently underwritten by the kings and consequently the forests often became nearly their private domains. In a technical sense they did not exercise hunting rights in the forests, but practically they did control the use of the woods in all ways, including hunting in them.[12]

Forest wardens were appointed under both Richard I (1188-99) and John (1199-1216) and were given great powers over game law enforcement. The first great English bureaucracy grew up in this area of governmental control. Under the wardens came chief foresters, baliffs and stewards. Laws gave an excuse for the creation of administrative rules which were promulgated by the forest bureaucracy and enforced with all the power available to these bureaucrats. Bribery was comon as a method of obtaining hunting privileges. The power of these offices provided many opportunities for corrupt officials to participate in graft. In short, the system was open to a great deal of abuse.

Complicating the system even more was the fact that the clergy operated under a wholly different law. The hierarchy of the clergy in England enjoyed most of the hunting privileges of the aristocracy. Those in positions of power controlled the lands that the Church had come to own and often forbade the common priests and monks to hunt. The bishops and others in high Church position frequently hunted and many kept falcons and hawks. These privileges continued unabated until well after the break between Henry VIII and the Roman See.

The right to "empark" or build walls or fences around a portion of the forest was given to those owning lands, whether clergy or nobility. The Norman kings issued two kinds of hunting permits. The landowners could pursue beasts of chase; these privileges belonged to the regular order of landowning prerogatives. The right to hunt beasts of the venery could be granted to others, with or without title. Beasts of the chase were hunted with the pack and included fox, marten, roe-deer, and fallow buck. The beasts of the venery were har, hind, hare, bear and wolf. Most of the hunting of beasts of the chase took place behind the enforested walls, a practice that the nobility equated with spreading and establishing one's domain. Within the King's forests, a grant to hunt beasts of chase might be given, but the hunting of beasts of the venery was only rarely given on the King's lands.

Commoners frequently poached on the King's lands or in the enforested areas of the noblity and were, under Norman law, severely punished. A semi-legal way of poaching involved luring the animals out of areas wherein the hunter could not pursue game into legal hunting areas. This form of poaching seems to have been common and brought about much friction between wardens and people.

By the time of Edward I Longshanks (1272-1307) the practice of forbidding hunting during breeding months was introduced into the law. During these "fence" months no one, not even a warden, could ordinarily hunt. This was a major step toward conservation and is evident in many other laws, including ones of contemporary vintage. These laws proved to be very difficult to enforce, especially in the more primitive areas of England. Similar laws are to be found in continental Europe. The general motivating influence in establishing these laws was toward guaranteeing that the kings and nobility would always have a supply of game to hunt. Even if done for the wrong reasons it still had a very positive influence on the development of a sense of responsibility in game conservation.

At approximately the same time wardens established breeding areas in which no one generally hunted. These might have been as elaborate as breeding areas set aside or as simple as creating banks wherein rabbits and hares and other small animals could breed. These fenced, banked enclosures for breeding were called "warrens." These could well be termed the first artificially established and maintained breeding stations.

After John Lackland's death in 1216 the laws of the forest were relaxed somewhat. No longer were poachers hanged or otherwise executed, and few persons were maimed after that. However, the punishment for hunting in the King's forests might still be meted out in many other ways, including fines. Also, the relaxation did not end the reprehensible practice of rendering a peasant's hunting dog lame by expedition. The clergy, as a law unto itself, continued to punish intruders in churchlands.

The simple and sad fact is that the nobility had placed great emphasis on the creation of laws designed to guarantee them a right over and beyond that of other men, and, to ensure this, had established a huge bureaucracy to create ever more complex rules and regulations. The medieval system of the hunt broke down precisely because it became overregulated and overbureaucraticized. This use of state power to regulate the many for the benefit of the few was doomed precisely because it was too complex. Too many exceptions were allowed, and, these being the prerogative of the sheriffs and wardens, too many opportunities for abuse, corruption, and malfeasance in office were permitted. It was one early, well-documented, and true story of the state being unable to regulate (with a welter of confusing and contradictory laws) what was unpopular in men's minds.

By 1139 the crossbow had come into general use in Europe. The pope in that year ordered that Christians not use it as the then ultimate weapon against their fellow Christians, although they could use it against heathen and pagans. But that prohibition served only to increase the popularity of that weapon. Deadly and silent, it had a range extended far beyond the other bows of the day. A hunter could silently poach on the closed forests of king and nobility. In a technological sense the crossbow killed off the effect of the remaining forest laws. Few noticed that death, for the laws had already suffocated under the weight of bureaucratic rule-making and regulation.

By the sixteenth century the gun had come into usage as a hunting weapon in Europe. Guns had been developed by the middle of the fourteenth century, but none of these primitive firearms had effective applications in hunting. A German manuscript of 1411 tells how a hand cannon was to be loaded and fired, but it is evident that the inaccuracy of these weapons precluded their use in the hunt. Early guns were designed to defend or to lay siege to fixed fortifications such as castles. During the Hussite Wars of 1420-34 smaller and somewhat more accurate handguns helped the Protestant forces of John Zisca defeat the finest Hungarian and German armies equipped with the ordinary weapons of the day. By the end of that war about one-third of the Hussite army had guns. Bohemian mercenaries became known as skilled gunners and, as a consequence, helped to establish the credibility of the firearm as a weapon of war. It was simply a matter of time until the firearm would be used regularly in hunting.

By 1475 the first true matchlock appeared. It was not the ideal hunting or military weapon because the fuse had to be lit and burning for the gun to fire. The life of a fuse was not long, so the gunner had to be prepared to light his fuse just before the target appeared. Premature and delayed explosions were not uncommon. The weight of the gun also dictated a rest, usually a forked post on which the barrel could be placed just before firing. The earliest hunting firearms in Europe and in the New World were matchlocks. The matchlock remained the standard hunting and warring firearm in both Europe and America until about 1700.

While the matchlock was designed primarily for warfare, and only to a limited degree for hunting, the later wheel lock was designed for, or at least used primarily for hunting. Leonardo da Vinci designed a practical wheel lock about 1508, but nothing was done about it until after his death in 1518. The first wheel lock was supposedly built by Johann Kriefuss of Nuremberg in 1517, but it is debatable because no record clearly established the latter's existence. One date can be established with certainty: Charles V of Spain had a wheel lock built before 1530. So effective was the new ignition system that the Hapsburg Emperor Maximilian I forbade the manufacture of these locks throughout the Empire.

The wheel lock was especially expensive to manufacture, and its life was tied essentially to sales to the wealthy. Matchlocks with extensive engraving and with carved and ornate stocks are the exception to the general rule. Conversely, it is most unusual to discover a wheel lock with a plain stock or without engraving. Some of the most beautiful craftspersonship in the world was lavished on wheel lock rifles and handguns. Many have silver, gold, and even platinum inlays or overlays in the metal parts, and stocks inlaid with precious and semi-precious materials. In short, while the matchlock was designed for the commoner and the military, the wheel lock was almost exclusively the hunting tool of the wealthy.

The matchlock was probably nearly as reliable as the wheel lock in military usage so long as the matches were kept lit. It was easier to care for, as the wheel lock's mechanism was delicate and almost impossible to repair in the field. It gathered dirt easily and a modest amount could incapacitate the mechanism. Considered as a whole, the wheel lock was slow to load; the mechanism had to be wound up like an alarm clock with a special key. Matchlocks were useless when the match fuse went out, while the wheel lock could be wound and kept ready for an indefinite period of time. Since a hunter could not guess exactly when game would be available the wheel lock was used for hunting whenever a hunter could afford one. The military had a much better idea when the rifle would be needed, and the limitations of the matchlock were not a great handicap. Also, a man whose fuse went out could usually borrow a light from his companion in the military, although that was not ordinarily feasible in hunting.

The nobility of Europe popularized the firearm, principally the wheel lock, as a hunting weapon. Had the hunter been forced to rely on the matchlock as a hunting weapon it is dubious that it could have displaced the crossbow. In the New World the wheel lock was more popular than the matchlock, especially after Amerindian tribes, one after another, learned how to neutralize the matchlocks. The Amerindians learned that the fires went out in rain, that the glow of the fuses made good targets at night, and that, on occasion, they could even trick the colonists into putting out the matches voluntarily. While other matchlock armed forces were occasionally defeated when caught with their matches out, the problem was more acute in the New World where the natives fought very unconventional wars.

In Europe the nobility hunted for pleasure and a shot missed because of firearms failure, whether of matchlock or wheel lock, was not anything more than an annoyance. Where one's life was on the line, whether because of Amerindians or because of starvation, men wanted more reliable mechanisms on their firearms. By the middle of the sixteenth century the flintlock, at least in primitive form, had emerged. The earlier forms, the snaphaunce and miquelet, were not as reliable as the later form, but they still outperformed the wheel locks and matchlocks. Although a few specimens of each were manufactured in Japan and in Europe until the end of the eighteenth, possibly into the nineteenth century, the flintlock was a system that satisfied the basic demands of low cost and great reliability.

As firearms came into use and became known as being superior to other weapons there were the inevitable efforts to control their use. For the most part these efforts were rooted in anti-democratic, reactionary thinking. If the people had not the means of liberal revolution they could be controlled. Some leaders thought to curb the rising crime rate by controlling firearms. Some thought to horde these newfound arms and protect these precious state secrets. He who controlled the firearms could control politics and history. Others thought that this special gift of technology was meant only for the nobility and was too important to be permitted to fall into the hands

of commoners. We must bear in mind that weapons had traditionally been ranked, so that one had to be of a certain class in order to
possess a certain weapon. Guns were the "best" and thus were
clearly to be restricted to aristocratic ownership.

Since, as we have seen, classes could hunt according to their positions in the caste, then it is reasonable to conclude that hunting weapons could also be apportioned by class. Again, firearms were to be
reserved for the nobles' exclusive use.

In 1548 King Edward VI of England sought to restrict the use of
what today might be viewed as a shotgun, then a novel weapon. His
act "against the shooting of Hayle Shotte" was designed to limit
firearms to single balls. The volleys that Hayle-shot allowed were
frequently directed at flocks of birds, whether in flight or on the
ground. Hayle shot was originally homemade by chipping lead
sheeting and then rounding it by rolling it around in some container.
The shot was loaded on top of a substantial powder charge with
some sort of wadding placed between the two. Since firearms at this
time frequently had barrels upward of a full inch in diameter, these
early shotguns could reek considerable damage. King Edward VI
suggested that the weapons were dangerous to both men (probably
the shooters) and animals, and they ought to be controlled.

With the advent of firearms, especially shotguns, man, for the
first time in his history had the means to kill off nearly any species
of game, including birds, that he chose. Heretofore, he had that
capability only in regard to the slowest moving animals, such as the
giant sloths or the Dodo bird. True market hunting of any kind of
game was now possible. This is especially true of birds, for only the
best shot could hit a bird in flight with a bow and arrow. Now, the
shotgun could drop a number of birds in a single discharge. Now,
man the hunter had to become man the conservationist or risk los-
ing all animal life.

The English as well as the other Europeans turned their attention
to studying the hunt and the rules under which the noble hunt might
be conducted. Some argued that the best hunt still was one in which
the old weapons, such as pike or crossbow, might be used by the
true gentleperson. Others argued that man might better again use
the power of the state to the advantage of the nobility and reimpose
restrictions on the general populace. Queen Elizabeth of England
(1558-1603) was a huntress who preferred the older weapons. It is
recorded that as late as 1600 she still rode her hunting steed and
killed animals with a crossbow. One of her favorites, John Selwyn,

is said to have been able to leap on the back of a fleeing stag, ride and direct it, and kill it with a sword or dagger at the Queen's feet. Other English nobility reintroduced the practice of releasing an animal (often hobbled) and having it chased by a pack of hounds. The Elizabethan hunters preferred to listen to the hounds in chase, rather than to use them to bring the game to bay and then kill it. When the animal was killed the act was frequently committed by a professional huntsman rather than by the nobles engaged in this form of the hunt.

While many early writers had offered opinions on hunting, it remained for post-industrial man to produce an abundance of literature on the subject. As early as 1275 *La Chace dou Cerf,* an anonymous manuscript, offered some perspectives on the ethics of hunting. But the impact of firearms on hunting brought additional literature. Charles IX (1560-75) wrote an essay, *La Chasse Royale.* Charles was an avid hunter whose premature death at age 24 was attributed to blowing his hunting horn too much. His work was, to some degree, a refutation of a much earlier manuscript, *The Statesman's Handbook,* by John of Salisbury. Salisbury had argued that kingly duties were so important that the prince should devote his full time to duty. Moreover, Salisbury had argued that one could not attain heaven if he was involved in such frivolous activities as dancing, singing secular songs, and hunting. Charles argued that it was perfectly natural to hunt and that this was a prerogative of the king who shouldered so many heavy burdens.

In 1561 another French book entitled *La Venerie* written by Jacques du Fouilloux offered the same perspective on hunting that we find in the essay by Charles IX. Indeed, some authorities hold that the book contained one or more sections written by Charles or plagerized from him. The book was a strong defense of the life of the idle, rich nobility. He encouraged kings and nobility to restrict hunting privileges to the nobility, and he thought of hunting noble animals as an activity fitted only to the nobles among men. He thought of medieval prerogatives to such a degree that he wrote of the desirability of having a young girl available for the pleasure of the hunter who was otherwise unoccupied during a lull in the hunt. The book did contain some interesting commentaries on boar and stag hunting, mostly with hand weapons.

The book appeared in an English translation, possibly done by George Turberville, the author of *Book of Falconrie* (1576). The book aroused some interest among the English nobility, but was unpopular with the commoners. One author suggested that it was the last book on hunting that could be applied equally to England and continental Europe. Still, the *Book of Hunting,* as the English version of du Fouilloux's work is known, was an anachronism. It did give useful insights into the decadence of the nobility which was gathered unto itself in a hedonistic existence totally oblivious to the humanity of the masses of men.

By the time of the ascension of the Stuart monarchy in England most of the desirable wild game had been hunted to extinction. Contemporary literature cried that there were more hunters than game. Fox hunting developed, partially because there was precious little other game that could encourage the baying of the hounds on the trail. Since much interest was focused on the hunt and the baying of otherwise rather useless dogs, it mattered little what the end result was. Hunters were not looking for a satisfying or inexpensive meal so much as for the sport of the chase. The classic fox chase thus became, to an idle nobility, a wholly acceptable pastime, and an acceptable relief from the boredom of a useless existence. It was easier to chase foxes than it was to restore true game animals. The last wild boar had been killed under Elizabeth I and so great an event was that kill that the name of the hunter, Sir Richard Grobham, is recorded for posterity.

In his work on hunting Sir Thomas Cockaine wrote of the increasing scarcity of various forms of deer. His *A Short Treatise on Hunting* (1581) notes the increasing dependence on the chase rather than on the hunt. He offers compensating features of the chase such as the whimsical musicality of the baying hounds. Cockaine noted that even hare and marten were growing scarce, so that hunting them was futile. Thus, eyewitness testimony suggests that overhunting, even when hunting is restricted to a privileged class, can ruin the hunt for all. The same law that restricted hunting to the few could have been used to limit their excesses when game became scarce. It is hard to find any justification for hunting animals to extinction and it is indeed a dubious honor to have one's name recorded as the hunter who killed the last of a native game species.

The English hunting law was designed to protect the hunting rights of the few, irrespective of the type of weapon to be used. It was not totally conservationist in that it was not designed to protect the existence of a species suitable for the hunt; rather, it was designed to protect an exclusive franchise of the wealthy and the nobility.

The continental Europeans did not see the folly of the English approach. They too hunted many species to extinction. They too refused to see that conservation benefits the nobility as well as the commoner. While some areas of Europe, notably Russia, had areas too remote to hunt to this degree, overhunting did occur in the Netherlands, Belgium, Spain, France, and Germany. In each step man was aided by the technology of the weapons industry. Firearms with rifled barrels proved to be much more accurate than smoothbore muskets.

Birds were generally not considered to be appropriate objects of the hunting carried on by the nobility, excepting those killed by captive birds of prey in that sport known as falconry. Ordinarily, the nobility did not attempt to hunt birds with bows or guns. Then, as the great and worthy animals disappeared, the nobility found that birds could be hunted with shotguns. Now, the slaughter that modern technology permitted became the sport of the nobles and the wealthy landowners. Beaters chased birds before them while gun bearers loaded gun after gun and the privileged shot birds in numbers heretofore unknown in the annals of the history of hunting. When these birds were reduced in numbers the wealthy frequently had aeries created wherein easily bred birds, notably pigeons, were raised especially for the slaughter. Live pigeon shooting, hardly either sporting or hunting, became a pastime of those who could afford it.

The debauchery that marked the English aristocrats' approach to hunting infected the continental Europeans as well. Hunting had become slaughter, a decadent spectacle. The true hunter disappeared with but rare exception. The low level of the behavior of the nobility in general can be seen in miniature in their approach to hunting. If it is true that King Louis XIV said, "after me comes the deluge," concerning economic and social policies, it can be said equally of the shortsighted policies he and his fellow aristocrats followed regarding hunting. No thought was given to tomorrow's hunt; it was today's pleasures that counted for all.

There are certain principles we can discern from our brief look at European hunting practices. We can see that evil men can manipulate the law to suit their own ends and that law can become a tool of the power structure. We see that conservation laws are only rarely passed by disinterested individuals. Most such laws are promulgated for reasons that are wholly self-serving. Properly directed, such laws can benefit both man and the animals, the hunter and the hunted.

Improperly directed, these laws have no good effect on protecting animals and an almost equally evil effect on men themselves. Good laws, dealing with conservation and hunting, and with many other themes, are rare. Indeed, they are as rare as good laws on anything.

Man can be counted on to do what is easiest. He may hunt with no thought of tomorrow, or he may be disposed to think of the future. Often, man sees an abundance of game and approaches it as an object of slaughter, rather than of the hunt. He may exterminate, or nearly exterminate, a species unless good men restrain him with good laws. He blusters about, giving no thought of what a species may require of man before it can be properly hunted. The Englishman hunting the marten or hare or boar to extinction has much in common with the American who hunted the bison and the cougar and the mountain lion nearly to the point of extinction.

Good laws made by free men, in a free environment with democratic implications, may mitigate against such excesses. Sport hunting can be protected for all more easily and more justly than it can be protected for the few.

The Amerindian and Hunting

The Savages take better care of us French than of their own children. From us only can they get guns. *(Sieur de La Salle)*

The American native, commonly called today the "Amerindian," is often depicted as the brother of all that lived. He was not considered, in his legends, to be wholly a different species of being from the animals he hunted. He shared this unusual view with very few other ancient people, notably the Egyptians of the classical age. In the conventional picture of the "white man's Indian,"[1] he is shown communing with nature, and with his deity through nature.

Animals were supposed to be sacred to the Amerindian.[2] Their sacred character was derived not from their being an incarnation of some or another god or goddess, but from the fact of their existence in nature. Some animals were closer to some tribes and hence these species became the object of the Amerindian's veneration. Animals were not gods in the sense of being a part of elaborate hierarchy of gods and goddesses. In general, a species of animal was not sacred because some or another god or goddess was wholly or partially a member of that animal species.

Animals had various traits for the Amerindian, just as they have in our common understanding. One speaks of the fox as clever and devious, or of the lion as the king of beasts, and the like. If a particular group of Amerindians found that a species of animal could be said to have certain values that the tribe held in esteem, then that animal might be given special consideration. Perhaps by communing in one way or another with that species, the Amerindian might acquire the desired virtue.

As with all primitives, the Amerindian assumed that traits of an individual or species of animals might be imparted by devouring the flesh, or by eating only a prescribed portion of the individual of the species. Thus, animals more highly valued than others were more frequently hunted and eaten.

The original legends of creation in Amerindian mythology describe the Creator as making man a hunter and the other animals the hunted. It was then by grand and divine design that the Amerin-

dian played out the hunter's role. Equally trapped by fate, the game
had to submit to being hunted. It was a tenuous but meaningful
partnership of pursuer and pursued. So long as the man hunted
honorably and well, the animal accepted its fate.

The hunter was obligated to take only what he needed. He was
not to kill indiscriminately. He was not permitted to waste the meat
or allow any portion to rot or waste away. In this the hunter had no
choice, for it was given to him as a part of his role in creation.

The ideal situation is shown in the use of the buffalo. Its hide
made clothes and moccasins. Its meat was eaten. Its droppings
made fires. Its horns could be used as decorations in the hunter's
own dress or made into a variety of useful vessels. Its sinews could
be used as threads or for bowstrings. In short, nothing was wasted.
In turn the animal received a certain veneration as "Father
Buffalo." Its strengths were an inspiration to the young man. It
held an honored place in the mythology. Dances were held in its
honor and in recognition of its role in Amerindian society.

Only the men could hunt. Agricultural chores generally belonged
to women or to captives. This again was in agreement with divine
design. The women had their role as farmers and as domestics and
child-bearers. The men were fully cast in the hunter's role. Manhood rituals were established in large as a way to test a lad's preparedness for his role as hunter. Because animals had dignity, they
could be hunted only by brave men, that is, those who had proven
themselves in an elaborate test of forebearance, skill, courage, and
fidelity. It would have been an insult to one's brothers, the animals,
to send a weakling or a coward on the hunt.

A portion of the hunt was devoted to understanding one's prey.
One not only hunted a particular animal, he understood it. He had
to know its virtues and vices, its strengths and weaknesses, its very
being and essence. Amerindians learned or created tales about their
animal brethren. To be sure, some portion of these tales was created
in the same way Aesop created his famous fables; that is, Amerindians used animals to illustrate points to be made about individual
men without directly confronting them. The bulk of these stories
was designed to install a sense of brotherhood between man and the
animals.

We have come to believe that no Amerindian would kill game until he was in communion with that species.[3] Hence, education began
early and was imparted to the youth before they underwent the
manhood ritual. Old men were generally charged with keeping and

imparting the animal mythology. The assumption was really quite simple. One had to appreciate the source of his food, clothing, shelter, and the like before he could hunt and kill it. Otherwise one might not regard the animals as his brothers and kill wrongly. If one knew and loved them as brothers he would do only what was right.

Nature and its animals were supposed to be the standard of goodness for the Amerindian. All human behavior could be measured against nature and the animals in precise measurements. Animals were generally seen to be courteous, kind, loyal, strong, brave, reverent, clean, alert, and loving. Before taking an animal in the hunt one had to be prepared to attest to his own purity of heart. He could not kill that which was more moral than himself. This, of course, assumed an intimate knowledge of the patterns of moral behavior of the animals hunted.

Subarctic Amerindians were obsessed with the responsibilities that man and animal had to one another. The injunction against killing too many animals ranked as the first law that the Amerindian must obey. That he may be killed by a man who was his moral equal was the first law for animals. Thus the animal, when seeing that his meat, hide, and so on was needed by the true hunter, was required to voluntarily surrender itself to the hunter. A hunter or an animal which did not obey the law violated the rules of nature.

A meeting of the man's spirit and the animal's spirit had to take place. Thus pre-hunt ceremonies took place in nearly all tribes. A man was clothed in animal hide to represent the spirit of the species to be hunted. Other hunters communed with that spirit through song, dance, and other sacred rituals. The hunters conveyed their needs to the animal spirit while the animals made their sentiments known in return. Hunters agreed on a quota of the species to be killed, and that quota was not to be overfilled. The hunt thus took on a sacred character. It was religious in the sense that the communication was in fulfillment of requirements laid down by the Great Spirit. The communication of spirits was itself a way of communing, albeit indirectly, with the deity.

Hunters who had properly mastered the communication with the animals enjoyed the additional benefit of being able to talk to "animal persons." There was, of course, a personality enjoyed not only by each species of animal but by each individual animal. Animals as part of a continuum of which man was a part, even though he might be the superior part, had intelligence. Hunters could, through meditation and ritual, communicate with that intelli-

gence. Man was merely a higher intelligence with greater responsibilities than those animals of a lower intelligence. Animals and man
were parts of the same creation, alike fundamentally, different only
in degree.

Part of the social discourse enjoyed by man and his animal brethren was the hunt. While it may seem to us as an imperfect way of
communicating with one's fellow intelligent creatures, the hunt was
the Amerindian's way of communicating in the ultimate sense with
the animal kingdom. However, the animals took offense to the hunt
only when they were indiscriminately slaughtered.

There were only a few other rules imposed on the hunter in the
use of game. The animals did not like to be consumed by menstru-
ting women. They did not like to be hunted without being given
proper respect, as in the pre-hunt rituals. They did not like to be
hunted by those men who failed to address them properly and with
the respect due them as brothers. They did not like to be killed by
men and fed to the hunters' dogs.

Animals assumed that men would always approach them with the
proper respect. They assumed that men would communicate with
them whether or not they were hunting. They disliked any sort of
belittlement.

The Indian held Nature in high esteem because he had little choice
in the matter. Nature was a force beyond his comprehension and
surely beyond his power to control. He could not alter the relationship given by the Author of Nature in any way. If he violated the
rituals or taboos, he would be punished severely. There was little
that could be objectively called romantic about his view of nature
save in the hindsight of those who studied his myths.[4]

If the Amerindian violated the tenuous relationship with the
animals they were free to ignore him. They could avoid his traps and
snares. They could remove themselves from the hunting grounds so
that even the most skilled hunter would fail to find enough food to
feed himself and his family. The Amerindian believed that there
were other weapons in the animals' arsenal. They were the carriers
of disease, pestilence and plague. They would bring about disease
and famine only when their dignity had been insulted by the
hunters. Animals also possessed magic to the degree that they could
render a hunter's weapons useless in the hunt.

The Amerindian's view of disease was the most interesting aspect
of the chastisement that animals could wreak on the discourteous
hunter. He had no idea of the nature of disease so he was an easy

victim of superstition. Disease was a punishment for transgressions against his animal brothers. They were the keepers of this potent weapon but were not permitted to use it unless the Amerindian had committed a grave miscarriage of justice against Nature. Therefore disease was proper and fitting retribution for not being in harmony with the laws of Nature. The solution to the problem is internal. The Amerindian had to right himself with the basic and natural forces that controlled his destiny.[5]

Game was generally plentiful, and the Amerindian generally kept himself in harmony with Nature's laws, if only as a matter of necessity. Early explorers found that squirrels were so plentiful that, on a trip from the east coast to the western slope of the Appalachian mountains, they had no difficulty in supplying themselves with meat. Several reports told of river travel on the Mississippi being held up by the quantities of game animals swimming the river. Deer, buffalo, bear and rabbits were generally available in significant quantity. Why then did the Amerindian violate the partnership with Nature with the coming of the white men?

The answer is found in the Nature of the Amerindian's life, rather than in his religion and his philosophy.[6] The Amerindian lived an essentially nomadic life. He had no reason to accumulate goods. He seldom stored goods for future use. Only rarely would the Amerindian after a successful hunt prepare meat for long term storage. When other commodities were in season he seldom prepared for the future needs, concentrating instead on the here and now.

Other than providing for food, clothing and shelter of the most basic and primitive kind, he had no interest in conspicuous consumption and waste. What indeed could one do with a number of animal hides or a quantity of meat? He was ill-prepared to preserve the meat, and the hides in quantity were a burden rather than an asset. Beyond the liturgy of religious taboos he simply had no reason to slaughter large numbers of animals. Hence his conservation was far more based on pragmatism than on principle.

When the white man came bringing trinkets of various kinds to trade for animal hides and certain choice bits of meat, the Amerindian did not hesitate to violate his conservationist principles. The partnership was broken by the Amerindian out of simple greed. He wanted the consumer goods the white traders offered. He quickly forgot that the animal was his brother. There was no longer any meaningful discourse between man and Nature.

The Amerindian had never experienced such a wonderful array of goods before the arrival of the white man. His technology did not produce beads and baubles, iron knives and cooking pots, colored cloth and the like. There was an instant demand and it was a trader's market. Whatever the cost in the disruption of his natural philosophy, he was prepared to pay. His religion was altered by the appearance of even the most valueless of trinkets. He was prepared to barter away not only his animal brethren, but his land and hunting rights as well.

The fur trade was a paradox for the Amerindians.[7] There was a clash of ideals. The fur bearing animals, especially the beaver, were the spiritual wardens of the forest. They had communed profitably with the hunters over uncounted centuries. They had kept their side of the eternal bargain, willingly entering the hunter's traps or submitting to his weapons in modest quantities. But it was only through the indiscriminate slaughter of these animals that the Amerindian could obtain the white man's trade goods. The demands on these animals was, to say the least, immodest.

By the end of the seventeenth century most of the prime fur-bearing animals had been hunted to the point of extinction in the Delaware River Valley. The trade with the Swedes and the Dutch was extensive even before the arrival of the first major colonizing groups of whites. The European market was glutted with furs even before white trappers arrived in quantity to deplete further the hunting grounds of the beaver, fox and mink.

With the arrival of large numbers of whites came disease in heretofore unknown quantity and intensity. Smallpox, syphillus, typhus, and typhoid fever were unknown in the New World. Whole tribes were devastated. Some nations, such as the Mandans, were destroyed. The Amerindian assumed that his animal brothers were having their revenge for his violation of the divine accord. The Amerindian knew no cure for smallpox, influenza, or the plague. The justice of the animal kingdom was swift and harsh.

Existing Ojibwa and Cree sources tell of the sickness brought by the animals on their nations. They saw this as punishment for transgressions against nature meted out by the "animal spirits" of the offended wildlife against the hunters who had broken the laws of Nature. What other source could there be for pestilence and disease other than the mysterious forces of angered wildlife? The Amerindian was clearly imperiled by the wrath of the animals.

Since the animals were no longer his brethren, the Amerindian was now relieved of his obligations toward the animals. The ethic was forever fractured. It could not be patched up with a new dialogue. Indeed, discourse with Nature was now impossible. The Amerindian was to be forever punished for the greed he had displayed in willingly sacrificing his animal brothers to the white traders in exchange for their goods. The hunter and his family had lived since time immemorial without such goods, and they could have continued to do so after these goods were first offered to them had their faith been strong enough. It was for their infidelity that they were being punished, and for which their sons would be punished in the future.

Since he could not regain his lost innocence and reestablish his fraternal relations with the animals, the Amerindian was free to make war on Nature. This he did with a vengeance. He chose to fight an all-out war with the animal kingdom; perhaps by doing this he could prevent the animal spirits from destroying him and his people. There was no other choice possible. Thus, by the end of the eighteenth century, there was a cataclysmic war being waged in the forests and on the plains. Amerindian hunters tracked game, killing without mercy or concern for their former brothers. No thought was given to the welfare of the animals or the future of the hunt.

The Amerindian had bothered the beaver but little before the fur trade with the whites began. The beaver had built dams that were useful to the Amerindian villages. It was a totem to many tribes and often viewed as the personification of the animal spirit, or as the custodian of the woods. Because of the special position of the beaver as well as because of the value placed on beaver pelts, it was the most devastated of all game species. The beaver was supposed to commune in special ways with the hunters, and it was assumed that the beaver had especially deserted men as disease arrived.

At least one author[8] assumes that disease arrived before the fur trade began. He assumes that Norman, Basque, and other European fishermen had plied their skills in the North Atlantic for a number of years before trade contact was made with the natives. These fishermen, he holds, had infested the Amerindians with a variety of diseases before the hunters began to kill the game in large quantities. If this thesis is correct, then it follows logically that the game animals, not man, were the first to break the covenant. The Amerindian was unable to discover why the animals had suddenly turned on them, bringing disease and plague. Since the animals had, without reason, caused havoc among the tribes, it was only just that men should attack them as the only possible means of punishment for such injustices.

The diseases were contracted first by the natives living on the eastern sea coast, and spread from there inland. The interior tribes, presumably not yet involved in the fur trade, were caught unaware. They reacted in the primitive way by destroying the animals which, they believed, had brought mass death upon them without reason. The wildlife which had, for mysterious and inexplicable reasons, brought disease on man were now imperiled by man for their violation of the sacred covenant. As the Micmac nation remembered it, there was war against Nature personified in the beaver as custodian of the forest. In any event, the dialogue between man and the animals, heretofore his brothers, had ended.

With the breakdown of the dialogue between man and the animals, the whole structure of Amerindian religion and philosophy was destroyed. Some tribes still tried to communicate with the animals, but the communication was incomplete. The rituals of the hunt lost their meaning. The hunt was no longer a noble endeavor; rather, it was war for survival of the Amerindians. All that buttressed the other ideas and philosophies was based on an understanding of Nature and the animals who lived in natural settings. In short, the Amerindian religion was bankrupt.

Against this background the Christian missionaries entered the woodlands of North America.[9] They taught that the Amerindian religion was nothing more than a collection of myths and fables. Such superstition had failed precisely because it was grounded in error. Since it was obvious to the natives that the religion had failed, and that it offered no method of reestablishing the fundamental dialogue with Nature, they became willing disciples of the new religion.[10]

The hunt could never again be a truly sacred event. It was now a secular ritual that could be carried on without regard to the laws of Nature. There was nothing in the new religion that allowed for a sacred hunt or a sacred dialogue with the animals. Man was transvaluated and became a whole species quite distinct from the animal world. The new theology had no use for the worship of nature. No salvation was offered for the animals, for salvation was the exclusive property of man. No means of purgation or atonement for the havoc wrought by the animal kingdom was included in the new religious philosophy.

With the Amerindian experience, we see the great paradox of primitive man when confronted by those new and exciting things that he himself could not have, imagined, let alone created. He was willing to sell out his birthright for a few trinkets; or he was willing to blame the great evils of a new and horrifying experience on his animal brethren. In short, he wholly lacked perspective, and thus in the long run, he destroyed himself by harming and destroying those with whom he had had heretofore a reasonable and sound relationship.

We have a modern phenomenon, an observable situation. We need not speculate too long on these circumstances through the uncertain paths of paleontology, archaeology or anthropology. We have historical evidence of the situation from a wide variety of sources. The innocence of the past is forever gone. The Amerindian could not revert to the status quo that existed before he encountered the white man. Given time for consideration and reflection, the Amerindian might have chosen a far wiser course of action; he might have chosen to continue forever in his partnership with the animal kingdom.

Might the Amerindian of today choose the modern and civilized life? It is a moot question, for, once having burned his bridges behind him, he had no choice but to continue on his now predestined course. The larger question is: How many times has such an event occurred in man's past? It is especially likely that man, by warring on game animals, by taking more of a species than the species' survival would permit, by overindulging in the bounties of the land, has, many times in the past, forced himself into new ways of life precisely because he destroyed the old ways.

The pattern of the Amerindian may have been set thousands of years ago, then merely repeated over and over again by ensuing civilizations. When game became scarce, man had no choice but to seek alternative ways to survive. Because he over-hunted, man is no longer a hunter, dependent on game for survival. Or, again, other groups of men may have found some pestilence too great to bear, and they may also have struck out in blind rage against the very beings, the animals, on whom their existences had hitherto depended.

I do not contend that man generally chose to quit being a carnivore consciously; rather, I contend man became an omnivore, tending more toward life as a herivore, because it was now necessary to his survival. The conditions man set for himself caused him, wholly unconsciously, to become highly dependent upon the growing of crops for his survival.

Whether by grand design or not, man had likely moved toward some dependence on plant food long before he had forced himself to all but abandon his existence as a carnivore. The variety of foods that plant life offered would surely have been a welcome relief from a constant diet of animal flesh. Many were immediately available to him in season. Others had been chosen as man mastered fire and cooking. Undoubtedly, at times, plant food had been essential to survival in periods when hunting was highly unsuccessful. But, as man moved toward modern human qualities, he must have been interested in the possibility of variety in much the same way you and I enjoy french fries with a steak.

The Amerindian was extremely fortunate to have had the American bison as a principal object of his hunt. Nowhere else in the primitive world was so much high quality protein available with such little effort. Despite his extremely extravagent way of hunting the bison, often driving whole herds over a cliff at one time, the Amerindian seemed incapable of destroying all these magnificent creatures. But even with vast quantities of bison available, the Amerindian added the variety of which I have just written by occasional planting and gathering of vegetables and nuts and berries.

So long as he controlled a hunting ground, the Amerindian had no need to advance to any higher level of civilization. His primitive weapons and his mastery of fire provided the wherewithal to feed himself well. Although he might waste some bison meat, and occasionally waste some other meats, he had no reason to destroy any other species so long as the partnership worked. The Amerindian remained primitive until after the white man's slaughter of the bison forced him to change his way of living.

Thus, the disappearance of hunting as the basis of a whole life style was a mixed blessing. It forced man to give up a way of life that had been traditional among primitive peoples for over two million years. It also started him on the road to civilization. Man the hunter would always linger around the twilight of civilization and recorded history. Man the planter founded cities and political systems and religions and cultures. But, deep within, there lingered a strong, instinctive desire to be the hunter.

One other conclusion is inescapable: man the primitive hunter was not merely a creature of nature living in a state of natural bliss with all the creatures of the forest. Man had a tenuous relationship that could be, and at least once was, broken for less than acceptable reasons. The Amerindian was willing to destroy his animal brethren for a few trinkets, provided he could rationalize an explanation for his change in hunting habits.

Primitive man did not work to ensure the survival of his animal brethren. He hunted, and, ordinarily, tried to avoid waste. But, if he could take more than he needed and blame it on accident, as in the classic bison drives, he did so. There was simply no inducement to extravagance, at least until the white man's trade goods arrived.

The Amerindians, or perhaps pre-Amerindian humans, did indeed destroy whole species of wild life. These were the animals that could fall prey to man easily, like the giant sloths. These primitive people had no game management plans. There is not a shred of evidence to impel one to conclude that the Amerindian would have taken actions to prevent annihilation of a type of animal.

In America, an abundance of game combined with a relatively small population of technologically backward people to encourage survival of most game species. This was not the case in other areas of the world. Larger populations, greater weapons sophistication, and less desirable areas for game combined elsewhere to force man from his hunting life.

America moved from such a lifestyle with lightning swiftness after the white colonists arrived. Modern technology wiped out the beaver, all but causing it to become extict. Within a few hundred years — a moment in the two and a half million year history of man — man could no longer ordinarily live here as a hunter. But in the long history of mankind, we were relatively slow in forcing ourselves to choose another way of life. All that remained was the latent desire to hunt.

Hunting and the American Experience

When Cortez began his filibustering expedition to the new World he brought with him thirteen guns. The firearms Cortez used were primitive and gave little technical advantage to the Spanish explorers over the traditional hand-weapons such as swords and bows. The matchlocks of the era weighed from fifteen to twenty pounds, and the matches, a kind of rope ignited to set fire to the powder in the guns, burned only a few minutes before burning out. The arquebus was a lighter and somewhat less effective weapon; it weighed only about eight to ten pounds. The Pope had no objection to the use of such unchristian weapons for hunting or against savages.

The Spanish were set on plunder, and most of their expeditions were mounted to find gold, silver and other precious objects. They sought the "seven cities" of the New World wherein valuable objects were said to exist in unlimited quantities. Cortez and his successor, Antonio de Mendoza, had outfitted several ill-fated expeditions in the 1530s. Even more elaborate expeditions took place under Francisco de Coronado whose retinue included 225 mounted horsemen, 62 foot soldiers, 800 Indians, and 100 slaves. Coronado returned to Mexico City in 1542 without having achieved his goals. It was not until Mendoza was replaced as the Spanish viceroy in Mexico in 1550 that the idea of rich cities still awaiting discovery was abandoned.

Between Cortez's first American expedition of 1519 and 1550 the Spanish armies had visited most of California, the American Southwest, and a significant amount of the Midwest. In general, the armies were equipped for war, for resistance was expected on the scale encountered in the conquest of the Mexican and Latin American wars. In actuality, few battles took place. The firearms were more generally used for hunting.

As expeditions bent on plunder became less frequent, the Spanish priests moved into the newly explored areas. They were interested in converting the heathen and establishing missions and towns. Towns such as Santa Fe were founded by large numbers of soldiers who had deserted or retired from the armies. By 1680 the mission towns with priests, a few slaves, Amerindian converts, and a handful of army retirees, stretched from Monterrey to the Conchos River through New Mexico and had reached the Pacific Ocean at the Sonora River. By the end of the sixteenth century the Spanish had successfully introduced sheep farming in the El Paso area. From 15,000 to 25,000 sheep were sold annually by 1620. The sheep adapted quickly to the sparse grass of the Texas ranges, thereby limiting the indigenous wild animals. Horses and donkeys that escaped from the settlements or from the explorers multiplied, again threatening the range and the food supplies of native animals.

The Spanish had been forced to bring cattle along with their invading armies because local wildlife that was edible by Spanish standards was rare in the area. What game there was escaped the efforts of the armies and settlers. Coronado's expedition of 1540-42 required that meat be carried along. Several expeditions failed because they did not meet their supply ships, or because they had counted on living off the land in an area where the land could not support even the native Amerindians.

In the Southwest the land supported only creosote bushes. The native tribes of Amerindians — the Bannock, Shoshoni, Ute, Paiute, Gosiute, and Suake — could barely eke out a subsistence level existence. The Spanish armies were unable to extort additional food from them, and eventually came to believe that the abject poverty seen among these aborigine was real. The Amerindians lived on grasshoppers, snakes, vermin, rodents, and any other small game they could capture. Such animal life was not to the liking of the Spanish, and quantities to support armies were simply not available anyway. The armies complained about conditions bitterly and were pleased to hand over both the land and its wretched inhabitants to the priests and missionaries.

While California may be viewed today as a land of milk and honey, such was not the condition when the Spanish arrived there. There were probably not more than 150,000 Amerindians in that province in 1600. The scarcity of natural foods forced the natives to exist in tiny bands which were notable primarily for their linguistic diversity and for their constant tribal warfare. They lived in simple homes made of brush constructed in the manner of a lean-to. Like most of the Southwest tribes they ate nearly anything they could capture, and their weapons were among the most primitive of any of the North American tribes. Only in the northern portions of the Pacific coast side of California were more advanced and prosperous hunting tribes encountered. The lack of significant quantities of rainfall made game scarce even in the now prosperous Sacramento and San Joaquin River valleys.

The general undesirable character of the Spanish possessions in the new world were their principal protection. No other European nation was interested in controlling the sagebrush and creosote bushes or the impoverished natives. This area of the American frontier was in large preserved because it was inhospitable.

The English in their search for a Northwest Passage invaded California as early as 1579 when Francis Drake's ship, the *Golden Hind,* landed at "New Albion." The Spanish realized the uselessness of the desert and semi-arid regions of the American Southwest, but they encouraged the establishment of colonies in these areas primarily as a first line of defense against incursion against Mexico. The search for areas suitable for colonization led the Spanish northward and to the selection of sites where natural resources were more abundant, such as in the San Francisco and Los Angeles areas.

The Spanish were checked in their expansion by the French more effectively than by the English or the Amerindians. Between 1685 and 1687 a French expedition led by Robert Cavelier, Sieur de La Salle, entered Texas in search of the Mississippi. La Salle's venture failed when his soldiers rebelled, but the Spanish did not find this out until 1689. By 1699 the French controlled what is now Louisiana and with it the mouth of the Mississippi River. The Spanish king was Philip V, the grandson of France's Louis XIV, and so he took no action against his grandfather. By 1719 the Spanish had been checked in their northeastern expansion by the French and had begun to retreat. A major defeat of a Spanish army under Pedro de Villasur in the summer of 1720 damaged the northern Texas defenses of Spain, and the French capitalized on the weakened perimeter. Thus the Spanish were contained and confined to the poorer hunting areas of Mexico and the American Southwest.

By this time both English and Russian expeditions had established control over the better hunting and trapping areas of the Pacific Northwest. Spain had been weakened at home by the catastrophic loss of the Armada in 1588 during its war with England. The Spanish never fully recovered from that defeat, economically or militarily. All told, the Spanish influence over hunting in America was not great. They were never successful as hunters or as trappers, and there was no substantial fur trade at any time with the Amerindians. The Spanish sought gold, not areas in which they could settle surplus population. The area they controlled did not invite colonies and this merely buttressed the prevailing sentiment that colonies were to be controlled not settled.

Had the lands in America been more hospitable perhaps Spanish colonies might have been established. The European settlers elsewhere were able to subsist because food supplies were not a major problem for the sponsors of the colonies. The colonists could kill the wild animals and sustain themselves if the supply ships from Europe were late. They could trade with the natives who had food surpluses. They could learn from them techniques of hunting and trapping. These things were not possible in New Spain.

Where the Spanish failed in the New World, the other Europeans succeeded. The French, Dutch, and English settled on the Eastern Seaboard of Canada and the United States; they soon established successful colonies and fur-trading posts. Their weapons, primitive by modern standards, provided sufficient firepower to kill even the largest species of game.

The French brought the matchlock to their new empire in North America in the 1530s. They used the matchlock and its lighter counterpart, the arquebus, extensively in hunting in the new world. The arquebus had somewhat greater appeal because it required no forked rest as did the heavy matchlocks. The records of the expeditions of Jacques Cartier (1534) and Sieur de Pontgrave (1603) show that these firearms were used extensively to hunt larger game and to impress, perhaps frightening, the Amerindians they encountered. Samuel de Champlain (1609) carried the arquebus in hunting with the Iroquois during his expeditions in the Midwest. The friendly tribes immediately sought ownership of these very impressive weapons, partially as a means of war, but mostly as hunting weapons.

The Dutch who arrived in 1613 on the Hudson brought with them the matchlocks that had by that time been standardized for use in the army. These weapons weighed approximately sixteen pounds and fired a .66 calibre bullet in a .69 inch bore. Their arquebuses weighed in some six pounds lighter and fired slightly lighter bullets. By 1656 the Dutch musket trade had reached such proportions that the government ordered that only whites could own such weapons and that further trade with the natives foreshadowed possible misuse by the Amerindians. Although the proscription carried with it the death penalty for violations, it was not successful in stopping the trade. The Dutch government then ordered that colonists could possess only matchlocks, proscribing the ownership of the more advanced flintlock weapons in the New World. After the Dutch government in New Netherlands was defeated by the Duke of York, the English attempted to stay the musket trade with the Amerindians, but they had no greater luck in the Hudson River Valley than the Dutch had had. The Swedes had brought their own version of the matchlock, and they also failed to arrest the trade with the Amerindians.

The French saw the musket as a major source of trade with the natives; as a consequence they never attempted to prevent that trade. By the 1640s the French government had begun to produce the flintlock musket in quantity, and many were shipped to the new world expressly for trade with the natives. So complete was the conquest of this new technology that by 1670 the matchlock was wholly obsolete, as was the arquebus. The matchlock was too cumbersome to attract much interest among the Amerindians. It was too complicated, too easily put out of commission, and too slow to load to hold the natives' interest long. In most ways the bow and arrow was superior to the matchlock. Certainly, the European crossbow was a more formidable weapon. The French rightly concluded that the matchlock could be traded to the natives without grave danger to the colonies. But an improved weapon — the flintlock — that weapon could indeed be both a major trade item and a formidable weapon that could be directed against their enemies.

The flintlock gun quickly became a primary trade item among the wares of the French traders. By the 1650s the French were able to do considerable business with the Amerindians of the interior. It has been estimated that in the mid-1650s there were about 150,000 Amerindians in the Great Lakes-St. Lawrence River area of whom about 35,000 were warriors who might potentially purchase French trade guns. Since the Amerindians could not produce shot, powder, suitable flint or ball, the trade was potentially open-ended. The French were less interested in living space than they were in trade, especially for the pelts of rare animals, principally the beaver, mink, otter, and fox. The simple way to approach the fur trade was with those goods that were in great demand. The gun, especially the new flintlock, was a status symbol for the warriors. It allowed the traders to carry one item — the trade musket and its supplies — that was a certain attraction to the natives.

The heavy muskets suited to army use on the continent were not to the liking of the natives. They rejected long and heavy guns that were most burdensome to carry through the woods on long marches. Consequently a unique firearm, the trade musket, was developed. This lighter construction allowed greater profits to the traders. A French *fusil-court, carabine* or *mousqueton,* cost approximately six dollars to produce. Records of the Hudson Bay Company show that this price remained constant for over a hundred years and that whether these guns were produced by English, French, or American companies the price changed little. These muskets were unrifled and thus not suited to long-range or precision work.

The price of guns was from two to fifteen beaver pelts, the fur trade standard of value. It sold for what the market would bear, and it changed in value according to the relative scarcity of beaver pelts. Powder was expensive, bringing from four to twenty dollars a pound, or in terms of beaver pelts, a pound of powder generally cost at least a pelt. Lead was traded at forty pounds for two to ten pelts, more if already cast in the form of bullets. Muskets generally fired projectiles weighing in at ten to twenty a pound. Black market prices, charges generally when a tribe was at war with the trading nation, were higher of course.

By 1618 the Iroquois had formed an alliance with the Dutch on the Hudson to obtain firearms in exchange for their furs, principally beaver. The related tribes such as the Erie, the Susquehanna and the Huron had established their trade relations with the French. By 1650 the Iroquois had, by and large, depleted the beaver supplies in their home and hunting areas. In order to satisfy their needs for Dutch, and, subsequently, English firearms they had to expand their trapping area into the lands traditionally held by their neighbors. The French could not support these territorial encroachments by the Iroquois and consequently they became bitter enemies of one another. The Iroquois expanded farther into the Midwest, making war on a number of tribes with whom the Iroquois had had only minimal contact heretofore.

The Iroquois had established an early and highly profitable trade with the Dutch, later replaced by trade with the English. By 1650-70 their homeland and hunting grounds were nearly depleted. Hence, they were motivated, perhaps determined, to expand their hunting area. Thus, they were faced with making the choice of either abandoning their newly acquired standard of living or making war against those tribes which had beaver in quantity in their hunting areas. Such loss of power and prestige was too bitter a pill to swallow for a proud and noble race such as the Iroquois. The whites were merely the unwilling partners in this dilemma. They did not drive the Iroquois to war. The relationship between the Iroquois and the Dutch-English traders was almost exclusively confined to trade in pelts. The Dutch were not interested in expansion against New France, and the English had not yet decided to use Amerindian allies against the French and their Amerindian allies.

The Iroquois attacked and stole furs from some western Amerindian tribes. These furs found their way to English merchants, not French traders. Had the Iroquois not stolen these goods the other tribes would have traded them to the French on the St. Lawrence River. To the extent to which the Iroquois were willing to trade with other tribes, rather than to make war on them, they acted as middle men, trading away from the French and toward the English. The Iroquois apparently had developed quite a profitable trade with some other tribes which made them wealthier than the other eastern tribes. But it also made them quite dependent on the nearest white colonies. Originally, these had been Dutch, and later English, but not French. The pelts had little value to the Amerindians, and so they had to trade them. The Iroquois wanted trade goods to barter with the other tribes and this made them dependent on the Europeans who had these goods. The Iroquois wanted additional firearms and the supplies necessary to work their guns, and this created a dependence on the English merchants and traders. The English were closest at hand, but they won out also because they were ordinarily willing to trade with the Iroquois on terms more favorable than those granted by the French.

There is a report that in 1681 the Iroquois had engaged in war with Illinois tribes over beaver hunting rights. Some forty or so Iroquois were killed in the initial hostilities which began as a result of a dispute over the ancestral hunting grounds. There are other reports of the Iroquois making war with the Algonquins and the Huron over hunting rights. The evidence is compelling that many Amerindians wars of the seventeenth and early eighteenth centuries were fur trade wars having their genesis in the expansion of Iroquois territorial and hunting rights. There is compelling evidence that leads one to conclude that the frontier wars between the French and their Amerindian allies on the one side, and the British and their aborigine allies on the other side, had their origins in the fur trade wars fought among the Amerindians even before the Europeans became involved. While it would be foolhardy indeed to suggest a single cause to wars such as the French and Indian War, there is strong evidence to show that one of the principle reasons for such wars can be found in Amerindian inter-tribal competition for pelts. The alliances of Amerindian tribes with Europeans were determined by fur trade partnerships.

Against this background some tribes struggled valiantly to maintain their traditions and their heritage. They eschewed the white man's trade goods. But these tribes were, by and large, subdued by the stronger eastern tribes who were backed by the white man's guns and steel knives.

One might conclude that the western tribes had a somewhat stronger religious orientation than their eastern brethren, for the western tribes resisted the threats to their ideals more strongly than did the eastern Amerindians. The hunting ethic was maintained until the bitter end. They were much more unwilling to participate in the wholesale slaughter of their animal friends. The eastern Amerindians showed a remarkable ability to dispense with the hunting ethic, trapping and killing animals in numbers far exceeding their actual needs. It is possible that the eastern tribes found their religion to be insufficient to provide an explanation and solace in a world turned upside down, perhaps a world gone mad, and they thus abandoned their religion.

On the other hand, the western tribes were pressed, first by their Amerindian brethren, and, only secondarily, by the whites. They apparently suffered less from epidemic diseases. The crisis period was longer and the exposure to white men was less immediate among western tribes.

It remained for the white man to move westward and to clear and farm the land and to destroy the animals which stood in his way before the western tribes would abandon their traditional hunting ethic completely. Many western Amerindians continued to commune through animals with nature long after this religious practice had been discarded by the eastern tribes. But the inevitable westward migration of white civilization would change the Amerindian's way of life forever, whether for better or for worse.

The frontier promised hope for Americans who wished to change their lives and fortunes. For the daring and resourceful individual the frontier promised much. Its egalitarian tendencies promised equality for the downtrodden. Its rich and unexploited resources offered a means to get rich beyond the expectations of city life. For the fundamentalist it offered communion with God and the creation first hand. Since most men were farmers anyway, the frontier promised ownership of land.

The easiest way to accumulate property was to obtain meat by the simple act of killing those animals which lived in the region. No foresight or planning was necessary. One did not have to cut away trees or prepare the soil well in advance. Rather, one picked up his rifle and went out into the woods where game was plentiful and shot whatever he wanted to eat. Secondary benefits accrued to the hunter. Animal hides were useful and they represented a basic storehouse for one's wealth. Much of the frontier priced goods according to animal pelts. These pelts could be traded for any goods the frontiersman desired.

There was no partnership with the animals. There was no religious sanction necessary in the hunt. It was a simple act of survival and of the accumulation of wealth, no more and no less. The animals were a part of the whole of nature. They had been placed there, presumably by Nature's God, for the unlimited use of men.

The Bible had admonished man to have dominion over the animals. He was enjoined to subdue nature, not live in harmony with it. It taught him that he was qualitatively different from the animals, superior to them. There was no reason to limit the kill and no reason to delay a hunt. The Bible was replete with stories of mighty hunters of ages past. The frontiersman was doing a natural thing when he exploited those resources that God had placed within his grasp, and those resources clearly included animals as they existed free and wild in nature.

There seemed to be an almost limitless supply of animals in the forests and on the plains of the new world. Squirrels were reported to exist in such numbers that when they swam across rivers they blocked passage for hours. Flocks of doves and carrier pigeons seemed to be without number. Deer existed in plentiful quantities. Elk herds numbered in the thousands. Smaller game and other birds lived in quantities that defied man to count.

As the fur trade which preceeded the farmers killed off such animals as the beaver, mink, and otter, other animal species seemed to multiply to take their place. Even these fur-bearers were not made extinct. They were now merely rare. Their numbers no longer justified large-scale trapping, but the frontiersman might still collect enough of these hides to make his efforts worthwhile. Where the trapper depended on fur-bearers to provide his whole income, these same animals represented a convenient supplement to the farmer's meager income. The trapper had been limited in his selection of species to those that offered high process because of the transportation problems. He could ill-afford to bring in deer hides, for example, because they fetched too little in the market to justify carrying them several hundred miles by horse or mule, by boat, or on his own back.

Hunting was such a necessary part of frontier life that the frontiersman of necessity became an expert shot. He had precious little ammunition to waste on target practice, but that enforced thrift caused him to learn quickly and well. The frontiersman was a true skilled hunter. The settler and his family had to depend on these skills merely to survive, especially if their crops failed. With game so plentiful the meat they supplied was the staple of life on the frontier. As construction of all kinds inevitably followed the settlers the construction workers were supplied with the meal of the wild animals by professional hunters on a regular basis. As with the farmers, the construction workers' preference for wild game was an economy. it was much cheaper to finance a hunt than it was to ship in domesticated animals or vegetables. There was not much incentive to raise animals for meat when wild game could be obtained so easily.

A hunter and his family might easily kill several dozen larger game animals and a hundred or more smaller species of game over a year. William "Buffalo Bill" Cody earned his nickname by killing 4280 bison over an 18 month period in supplying railroad construction workers in 1868-69. In the 1870s ranchers and workers in Arizona survived on antelope meat.

By traditional standards, Americans did not hunt, they slaughtered. The skill required was minimized. A day's hunt would ordinarily be successful. Game had generally not developed much sense of survival. Many of the principal objects of the hunt were unprepared to offer resistance. Man's technology had extended his effective hunting range almost beyond the conception of the only hitherto existing hunters, the Amerindians. Although many game animals had developed a sense of distance vis-a-vis the aborigine's arrows and spears, they had not developed an adequate sense of distance vis-a-vis the white man's guns.

Man at this point could hunt with relatively little skill. He did not enter the woods to find one specific quarry; rather, he entered, as had his ancestors of the Paleolithic Age, merely to find some meat. He could be selective in the kind of meat he chose, say, buffalo instead of rabbits. But he was merely hunting with no thought of sport.

America proved to be a throwback, then, in an otherwise rather orderly progression away from meat hunting and toward sport hunting. The philosophical and moral overtones were once again passed over in favor of raw, primitive survival. The romance of the hunt disappeared.

Animal life had no sacred character to it. It was merely a part of a grand totality to be subdued and conquered. Rules that had been brought about and enforced during thousands of years of relative scarcity were thrown out. Such rules no longer had pragmatic value. Animals were merely something to be used in any and all ways that suited man. The analogy was clear between the scarcity-caused and enforced conservation of trees in those areas civilized man had long inhabited and the indiscriminate cutting of vast, priceless, virgin forests on the one hand, and the change in man's hunting habits, from limited to unlimited hunting on the other hand.

Animals were also an impediment to progress. Wild animals ravaged plowed and cultivated fields and orchards. The larger predators threatened man himself. Since these animals were considered to be limitless in number, one might well consider clearing them as he had the forests.

This ecology of abundance, encountered nearly everywhere in the United States and Canada, save for areas of the Southwest, was something wholly new to man. He had not known that such quantities of game could exist in one place, let alone everywhere. He did not know how to behave. His actions proved this. Rules that have no rational base are discarded or ignored. Against this new background, all the old rules of conservation were ignored. And man seemed not to suffer for his waste and his slaughter of the animals.

The change of land usage accounted at least as much for the great decimation of the once limitless game herds as did hunting. Farms and range use rendered the bison obsolescent. The grand stands of trees were no longer there for the squirrels. Domesticated animals which escaped and went wild competed against native species for forage and living space. That struggle continues today, as we see in the competition between wild donkeys and indigenous species in the Grand Canyon area.

The disappearance of the great bison herds was first reported by Fremont in 1835, long before the settlers or ranchers had made significant inroads into the bison grazing areas. Some species were thinned by the professional hunter who was interested only in small portions of the animals, usually the hide. The animals were simply one more resource to be exploited.

By 1840 most species of game that could be taken by snare or trap, and whose pelts were valuable, had been decimated. The last gathering of western trappers took place in 1840. After that time it was no longer profitable to trap for beaver, mink, or otter. The white trappers and the Amerindians had all but rendered these fur-bearers extinct. These trappers had not taken animals for their personal use, but had chosen to strip off the hides, leaving the rest to rot.

The bison were killed off for the tongues, hides and a few, select portions of meat. These professional hunters acted like slaughter-housemen. Buffalo hides sold for as little as $1.25 each in the 1870s. Tongues brought $.25 each. Portions of the hind quarters sold for only a penny a pound, hardly worth the trouble of butchering and bringing the meat to market. By 1885 the bison herds were gone. A naturalist for the National Museum, William T. Hornady, reported that only 1091 bison remained on the plains in 1887, with 250 more on private ranches. The end of the buffalo meant the end of the independence of the Amerindians of the plains. It also meant that the frontiersman could not gather meat easily for his family.

Other species of game diminished in number for different reasons. Despite heavy meat hunting of the pronghorn antelope, there were still significant numbers until the winter of 1893-94; but then over 80 percent of the pronghorns succumbed during that unusually harsh winter. Additionally, portions of their grazing land was taken over, primarily for sheep ranches. Many antelopes were slaughtered because they competed with the sheep or with cattle for water and pasture.

The mountain goat population has remained steady. Evidence seems to point to a rather constant population of 15,000. Expansion of the herd seems to be more limited by adaptability than by hunting. The moose also lived in limited ranges, mostly in Montana, Wyoming, and Idaho. It requires semi-aquatic conditions for a satisfactory life style, and its numbers in the United States were never significant. Mountain sheep succumbed to a variety of diseases, especially scabies, lungworms, and pneumonia. They would not coexist with mountain goats and seemed willing to allow the goats to take over their range.

When the Europeans arrived it was estimated that ten million elk lived in what is now the United States. Elk herds now number about 100,000. While the elk were hunted for meat, hides, and their canine teeth, the herds disappeared largely because of starvation. Their range was taken over for farms and homes. The forests that they roamed were cleared and the timber destroyed or used. By the 1870s the primary threat to the elk was starvation, not hunting.

Other animals were hounded by ranchers and farmers, not because they had any intrinsic value but because they were disliked. Bears, especially the grizzlies, were feared as were the big cats. Both were blamed for killing domestic animals. Some were alleged to have attacked and killed humans. The pumas, largest of all American cats, were supposed to be responsible for large kills of deer, elk, bighorn sheep, cattle, domesticated sheep, and assorted other animals. These cats were hunted, not because of the value of the hides, although they did bring good prices, nor for their meat, but because they were thought to be undesirable in a civilized world. Bounties had been placed on smaller cats, such as the bobcat, as early as 1727 and the bounty system continued in many states up to the present. Wolverines, called "skunk Bear" by the Amerindians, were feared also. The Hudson Bay Company bought the hides mostly as a way of establishing bounties on the wolverines. Between 1821 and 1906 only 101,426 hides had been purchased, averaging only a little over a thousand per year.

By the middle of the nineteenth century poison was already being used to destroy animal species that farmers and ranchers did not like. It was the common practice on the plains to shoot a bison and then pour strychnine over the body. This would kill some wolves, but it also killed fox, skunk, opossum, hawks, eagles, bustards, and ravens. Similar poisoning practices came into vogue as a means of controlling the wily coyote. Poison is used as a common control of wild animals in the west today.

Those animals that could not be controlled by poison were hunted in mass by professionals or ranchers. The prairie dog was a nuisance because it burrowed in the ground, leaving holes in which cattle could step and break a leg. Other smaller species were either just in the way of progress or inconvenient to man and hence exterminated.

As was the case with so many animals, many species of birds were caught in the unfortunate position of either being considered a nuisance or being marketable as edible meat. The classic case of the

latter condition is the carrier pigeon. It was found in huge flocks, so
intense that their flight often blotted out the midday sun. Their nesting grounds covered many square miles. But their flesh was a
delicacy and so they were shot by market hunters. Their nesting and
breeding grounds were taken over by farmers. Various types of wild
ducks, swans, and similar migratory birds were hunted by the
market hunters as well. Eagles and hawks shared a different fate.
They were believed to prey on domesticated animals and fowl, and
some were accused of carrying off children in their talons. These
birds, then, were simply destroyed.

The disruption of their native habitats probably destroyed as
many birds as did the hunters. Some birds, like eagles, have not
adapted to new conditions of coexistence with man. As the frontier
was pushed back the birds retreated until only a handful of condors
and eagles remained in North America, and these were primarily in
wilderness areas. Chemical pollution, some of which, notably DDT,
damages the eggs or reproductive systems of the big birds, has accounted for additional losses.

One can infer certain things about the pattern of hunting in
America. For the most part, species of animals were killed off
because they were incompatible with the drastic change in man's
lifestyle that accompanied the passing of political power from the
Amerindians to the Westerners. The Amerindian did little to change
the forest; Western civilization saw only change. Some animals
adapted while most did not. Some large animals and nearly all
predators were not given that chance. They were unwelcome in the
New World. One might allow rabbits and squirrels in New York's
Central Park, but it is unlikely that the city dwellers would want
deer, moose, elk, large cats, or bears roaming there.

The Amerindian could be controlled only when America
destroyed his food supply, namely, the bison. Thus, the government
encouraged the destruction of the vast herds as a conscious part of
its Amerindian policy. Even if it had been done in a less direct
fashion the simple fact remains that huge, roaming herds of bison
were incompatible with cattle or sheep ranching and with large scale
farming. In one way or another Father Buffalo's reign over the
prairies was ended when civilization appeared. Again, the meat and
hide hunters who slaughtered the bison were merely instruments of
more profound policy.

There is no certain way to prove this hypothesis, but it may have
been that the carrier pigeon could not have stood the shock of being

reduced in numbers from the flocks of millions to flocks of a few dozen. Its gregarious habits may have been too strong and, as a member of a small group, unadapted to life outside the flock. I believe that there is exterior evidence that such was the case. We shall never know for certain. What does appear reasonably certain is that farmers and others would not have tolerated the continued existence of huge flocks, which would have devoured immense quantities of food daily, and which would have been quite dirty. We can see the reactions of city dwellers to the comparatively small flocks of pigeons and the reactions of farmers to the again comparatively small flocks of crows, starlings, and blackbirds.

Without continuing to press the obvious point of the incompatibility of larger predators and cities, it is nearly as obvious that suburbanites and even farming and other rural families do not wish to have substantial numbers of these animals near them. The farmers of rural West Virginia, New York and Pennsylvania have, for many years, wished to reduce, not enlarge, the numbers of wild cats and bears. Generally, we will find these animals increasingly confined to national wilderness areas, and with good reason. Man continues to build up, populate, and civilize America at an unparalleled rate. A portion of this process includes the removal of most wild animals.

If only because America has such vast expanses of otherwise unused land we can expect public policy to continue to support the maintenance of wilderness and primitive areas. Hunting can be preserved as can animal species by maintaining such areas out of the reach of the developers and the urban planners. So long as we maintain farms we can expect as well to have significant amounts of land open to small and medium size game animals.

Americans have chosen not only to create significant preserves, but they have dipped heavily into their pockets to finance restoration of game species. They chose to do this before many species of animals had disappeared or had reached the point of no return from extinction. In the cases when species continue to exist at the threshold of extinction, it has not been because of human neglect; rather, it has been in spite of man's efforts. Some animals, notably bird species such as the American bald eagle and California Condor, have not responded to man's charitable attempts to save them.

Several efforts to save hunting are worthy of note. The American Wild Fowlers Society created a program to help breed more ducks in the 1920s. This was renamed More Game Birds in America Foundation and, in 1937, reorganized as Ducks Unlimited. Sportsmen, including many famous hunters such as Bing Crosby, Clark Gable, and Gary Cooper, have contributed many millions of dollars toward its efforts, which included buying or leasing breeding grounds. The Pittman-Robertson Act of 1937 was a tax program that sportsmen requested. An 11 percent excise tax on all guns, ammunition, and reloading components, including those used in recreational and target shooting, is collected and expended on hunter support programs. Some of that game conservation money has benefited game, and some has benefited non-game animal species. The Federal Migratory Bird Hunting Stamp Act of 1934 has provided additional millions of tax dollars for conservationist projects. These expenditures are over and above the hunting license fees collected in each state annually.

Is It Ethical to Hunt?

No issue has so captured the interest of Americans in the last decade and a half as that of firearms control. Since the assassination of President John F. Kennedy there have been hundredsof bills introduced in the United States Congress and many more into state legislatures to deal with firearms ownership and use. One of the principal reasons why Americans own and use firearms is to hunt animals. Many legislative proposals try to distinguish between those kinds of firearms one can use to hunt with and those allegedly designed only to kill other human beings. Other bills seek to outlaw the private ownership of all guns ostensibly in the name of "crime control"; however, these measures seem more to reflect a deepseated, moralistic antihunting, anti-gun sentiment labeling all guns "evil" because of their potential to kill—humans or animals.

Precious little attention has been focused on the development of a theologically based ethic of hunting. The supporters of hunting have given little thought to such an ethic. The detractors have sought to condemn hunting, generally along with firearms, without stating the origin or the meaning of their moral condemnation. The cause of a hunting ethic is drowned out by the shouts of those who would place the taking of animal life under the protection of the commandment that "Thou Shalt Not Kill."

There are of course certain religious movements among the many in man's religious experience that one would expect categorically to reject the hunting of animals. Certain primitive religions have found various animals to be the bearers of divine redemption. The ancient religions of the Near East gave such status to many of the native species. Hence the cat, the jackal and the hippopotamus became symbols of the gods, and one could never be certain that he was not killing one of the incarnations of those deities.

One would similarly expect the pantheist to reject hunting because of the relation of all living things to the divine. Wanton killing might in some way disturb the fundamental harmony of the pantheistic universe. The killing of an animal would be, at least symbolically if not actually, the killing of a portion of the godhead.

Again, one would expect that he who accepts reincarnation would also reject the killing of animal life. Since one might himself be reincarnated as one of the animal species, such killing would be symbolic suicide. Actually, the killing of an animal would be the killing of what was formerly and what might be expected in the future to become a human being. Thus, hunting is tantamount to murder.

Finally, there are those religions which have taught the basic brotherhood of all animate creatures. Although different from man, the animals were nonetheless his brothers. Hunting thus becomes fratracide. Such religions would not accept the fundamental and qualitative distinction between man and animal, between the human soul as an act of God's special creation and the principle of animation in the animals.

American society is fundamentally Judaeo-Christian in origin and in ethic, and it is easy to dismiss these ideas. If one is to try to construct a Judaeo-Christian ethic of hunting he must begin with quite a different set of fundamentals. He must look to Biblical teachings about the nature of man, of reality, and of God to establish his ethical presuppositions and predispositions.

Man is the focal point of visible creation. He is indeed fundamentally and qualitatively different from the animals of the forests and the meadow. He has a special place in the divine plan, a place that involves a far different end than that of the animals. Man is so much a part of a separate teleology in Christian thought that God chose to become man and to offer Himself as sacrifice to atone for the sins of man. Such theological teachings do not suggest that God chose to sacrifice Himself to redeem the animals.

God is the Creator of the universe and, with it, all reality. What God made, He made good. That the universe is dualistic, with the simultaneous existence of God-originated good and evil, is an unacceptable position. Man is at the pinnacle of the creation in this world. He was given full dominion over the animals and was ordered to name them according to the wishes of man. Man is fallen man. He can do both good and evil, and he is accountable for those evil deeds that he does.

Of all God's creatures, only Man is capable of sin. At least since his fall his deeds can be accounted as good and evil. Animals are amoral—that is, incapable of good or evil. No animal is capable of either a good act or an evil one. Only a human ethic can be applied to animals. Hence, one might say, "Good dog" in the sense that the animal performed according to that norm of behavior established for it by its master.

Sin is an act against one's creator or against one's fellow man. It is, in a sense, a denial of love or charity. In committing an immoral act one is saying that he does not love that fellow human or his God against whom the evil act has been committed. Sin thus implies a rejection of that level of creation which is above man or is at his own level. One does not sin against those beings lower in the creative hierarchy than himself. Thus, one does not sin against animal life.

If it could be shown that the killing of animals was against the law of God, then such killing could be condemned as sin for the simple reason that it would be an act of reaction against man's creator. However, as we have seen, this argument cannot be sustained in a careful reading of the Biblical texts.

Traditional philosophy distinguishes between classes of creatures. It notes qualitative differences between God and man, between man and the animals, and between animals and inanimate creatures. No philosophical distinction is required between warm-blooded animals and cold-blooded animals such as fishes. Philosophically and morally we need not look for distinctions between hunting and fishing in our search for an ethic of hunting. We may very well seek an ethic of the two together.

We have assumed that the Ten Commandments were created by God to establish norms of human behavior among humankind, and between humans and their Creator. Thus, we assume that the admonition not to kill implies only that we not kill one another. The killing of God would of course be a logical impossibility, since it would imply a contradiction, viz., that the Immortal God could die. The assumption then is that the killing disallowed by the Ten Commandments has nothing whatsoever to do with the taking of animal life. Any argument against hunting based on the Ten Commandments is necessarily based on a misreading of the language and intent of these laws.

Since there is a profound and fundamental difference between human life and animal life the idea of killing is only analogically applied to the two. The taking of animal life means only that the principle of animation is no longer in the animal. The taking of a human life means that the human soul is freed from the body and that it goes to another realm of existence, to be judged by the deity. It is against the arbitrary taking of human life that the Biblical injunction against killing is directed.

In the relationship between humans and animals one may find analogies to the relationship between the deity and his creations. Thus, in David's killing of a predator which was attacking his flock

one can suggest an archtype to Christ as the Good Shepherd protecting us humans as his flock. But such an analogy implies only a way of
looking at our relationship to God. It says nothing of hunting.

We may thus reasonably conclude that hunting in and of itself is
permissible as an activity in which the theist may participate. One
finds nothing to prevent it and much to support it as a worthwhile
human activity. However, inasmuch as it is a human activity it can be
regulated by ethical standards and mitigated by moral considerations.

One may not be permitted to destroy a particular species of animal.
This would not be a sin against the species itself, but it would be an
act against charity and love. It would deprive future generations of
the opportunity to view that animal, to observe its activities, and to
pursue and take examples for meat or for sport. Accidental destruction of an animal would carry no moral condemnation, for only a
conscious and willful act can be judged against a latitude of right or a
longitude of wrong.

One could argue that an entire species of animal may be hunted to
the point of extinction morally under certain specific conditions.
For example, the rat does considerable damage to the human being.
It carries a variety of diseases, and it eats food supplies needed by
human beings. Thus, one might well destroy the rat, unless some
additional evidence defending the rat were to come to light.

While one tends to think exclusively of larger animals, one may
note that scientists seek to destroy whole species of microscopic
animals. If it can be shown that a certain organism, which, by biological standards, is an animal, does grave harm to the human
being, say, by carrying disease or itself causing disease, one might
well destroy it. Perhaps in the process of mankind multiplying and
subduing the earth, as we are charged to do in Genesis [1:27] we
might eradicate both large and small animal species in order that
man might better survive.

One ordinarily assumes that the hunter will be a principal practi-
tioner of conservation. It behooves him to encourage the desirable
game species to multiply, if only so that they may be hunted. If an
animal is a particularly desirable creature because of its meat, because
of its trophy qualities, or because of its pelt, man might well make
every reasonable attempt to ensure its survival in numbers. This has
clearly been the case. In a number of programs hunters have sustained
programs that encourage the multiplication of animal species. One
such program, Ducks Unlimited, seeks to protect the nesting area of
many species of ducks and swans. The sportsmen, as early as the

1930s, sought an excise tax on firearms and ammunition, and the money was to be used to reestablish game animals in North America.

The hunter has an obligation not to waste what he has taken. He is not to kill more animals than he can use, and he is not to waste those animals he has killed. He is under an obligation to use as much of the meat, hide, and bone as he can. He may fulfill some obligation to charity to his brethren by giving them from among his kill.

The hunter who wastes what he has killed is guilty of sin, according to the setting. If game is scarce, or if some are in need, and he wantonly kills and wastes he will have committed an offense against charity. If, however, game is plentiful, and if there is no known need, he may not have sinned at all. In any event, it is doubtful whether his sin would exceed that of the individual who throws away good food when others are in need.

The hunter may not destroy the animals of others. As early as Exodus (21) the law proscribed men from injuring the domesticated animals of his neighbors. The offense was of course against property, not against the animal itself. In the Bible one is clearly directed away from offenses against his neighbor's property. The hunter must thus exercise caution in hunting that he not injure or destroy the domesticated animals of his host. He must respect the various improvements on the property such as fences and buildings. He would be under obligation to close the gates against the possibility that livestock may stray. He must recognize the fact that while wild animals themselves cannot be owned as they exist *ferrae naturae,* the right to hunt the game is a property right of the landowner.

The hunter would be under a moral obligation not to willingly hurt even wild animals. This would differ little if any from the obligation one has to his own human dignity not to harm or injure any animal willfully. A hunter who entered the woods with the idea of merely injuring the game he stalked would be in the same league as the man who ties a can to a dog's tail or otherwise willfully hurts another's pet. Again, the injury, as a moral consideration, would be to the individual himself and not to the animal involved. This is the potential evil of man's relationships with animals, that, due to a fault of man's character, he may use animals as a vehicle to express his sinfulness. The animal is wholly passive in the act of sinning. It is in the same moral position as the chair, or table, or other inanimate object that becomes the object of man's misbehavior.

A hunter may pursue the object of the chase with an attitude of hostility. Whatever its cause or its source, hatred necessarily brings with it injury to the hated and to the hater. There is always an element of evil in any hostile activity; it presents a clear occasion of sin. If man acts with hostility toward an animal it will necessarily be intentional hostility, and this threatens grave injury to the hunter.

There is an evil, or strong potential evil, in nearly everything man does. It is for man to work out his destiny, to bring conscious moral standards and principles to bear in his own life. If there is an innate hostility in a man, perhaps it is better that this be worked out against animals than against his fellow man. If man controls the hostility in his soul by venting it in a healthy way in hunting, perhaps he shall have grown spiritually for it. At the worst, since he can harm only himself in the occasion of the hostility-laced hunt, man shall have chosen the lesser of two evils in avoiding hostility vented at other men.

There is yet another evil with which man the hunter must contend. If, in the course of seeking his pleasure in killing animals he becomes sadistic, he can harm himself by giving way to unhealthy and sinful appetites. Man is called upon by Judaeo-Christian ethics to control sinful and degrading appetites. One may, in rare cases, develop sadistic patterns of thought, or participate in sadistic acts, while hunting. There is a minimal chance that man might move from practicing sadism against animals, degrading only himself, to practicing it against humans, thus sinning against them as well. It should, however, be stressed that this is an extremely rare circumstance, involving a tiny, almost uncountable, minority of hunters.

There is no evidence that man hones his sadism on the grinding wheel of the hunt. The assumption is reasonable that one who is prone to sadism, and who is unable to control this bizarre desire, will find an outlet of one sort or another, whether hunting is permitted or denied. In the study of sadistic murders in our society there is evidence that true, undisciplined sadists do not hunt as a less harmful outlet; they are much more likely to act directly against other human beings, entirely by-passing hunting.

It is again possible that man becomes so obsessed with the hunt that he forsakes other, more intellectually stimulating and rewarding activities. One can think of Melville's Captain Ahab pursuing the great whale, Moby Dick, without regard to cost or consequences. Like any human activity, hunting may be reduced to an obsession, thus bringing grave harm to the person. In misdirecting all of our energy to any one activity we limit our scope of action and reduce ourselves to a one-dimensional being. The possibility that hunting will become such an all-consuming fire is no greater than are the possibilities for working, eating or engaging in sex.

One can transvaluate his own role in society, in the state, or in humankind by misappropriating his time and efforts. One can, by becoming single dimensional, deprive society of one's talents or artistry. But the proper placement of man, the proper development of total values, is the proper subject for theological concern.

Within the context of Judaeo-Christian ethics we can conclude certain things about the hunt. The hunter may not kill more than he needs, unless there is an unusual quantity of game available, without violating love and charity toward one's neighbor. He may not hunt and kill game on another's land without violating God's law against stealing. He may not kill another man's animals for clearly stated Biblical reasons; there are both general prohibitions against taking or destroying another's property, and there are specific proscriptions contained in Exodus 21.

One may develop interpersonal contacts through hunting. One may choose to share his company, his knowledge, and his love with others in the course of the hunt. He may share the product of the hunt, especially with the needy, in fulfilling an obligation to charity. He may share hunting and shooting opportunities with others. He may develop a sense of love and company with his hunting party. The hunt may serve as a catalyst to bring men of good will together. It may become an event that serves to develop mutual respect and admiration.

It can become a reasonably ethical way of venting pent-up hostility. One may sin to a small extent in giving outlet to potentially sinful activity, but it is, relatively, the lesser of two evils, for the alternative is likely the venting of hostility on other humans. Hunting is also a way of developing a sense of communion with nature, and with God's total creation in a natural setting. It is a way of developing a sense of conquest of nature, of fulfilling Genesis in "subduing" the earth and the animals over whom man is given dominion.

The doctrine of sin, as it is conventionally understood in the ethics of the West, precludes man sinning against animals. Man can sin only against God himself and his fellow men. Providing that he conducts himself within reasonable, human, and ethical parameters, man does not sin in acting out the hunt and the kill to the fullest possible extent. In the final analysis, one must always judge the guilt (if any) against the motives. Even the most charitable act, if done for wrong reasons, can be sinful. Hunting, if done for right reasons, is sinless. If one moves away from the hunt as it is conventionally known, and chooses to act out unusual, unhealthy, or bizarre and sadistic fantasies, one may sin against himself, and, potentially against others. Such potential for misbehavior accompanies all human activity.

A hunter may pursue game as a means of obtaining meat for his family. The provision of sustenance for one's family is a moral action. In a moral hierarchy of hunting activities this would rank the highest, for it encompasses the noblest of all reasons for killing game. This would presumably be within the same sphere of activity as practiced by the mighty hunters who stood high in God's eyes. Likewise, a hunter who killed game to give to the poor would be engaging in a highly moral activity, one vitally interconnected with charity. There would be nothing morally wrong about trophy hunting. The hunter should presumably be under greater moral compulsion to make certain that he was not endangering a species of game, or taking merely for his own pleasure, what another needed for his sustenance. One who hunted for trophies only might well have to guard against the sin of excessive pride.

We thus conclude that hunting may be quite moral. We may apply Biblical admonitions to respect the property of others, to uphold the human dignity which we all possess, and to practice our obligation to charity in hunting. We can articulate a basic ethic of hunting within the context of Biblical teachings. Whatever ethic may be developed against hunting comes from outside the Bible and cannot be supported by the teachings of either the New Testament or the Old Testament. Such circumscription of hunting may be grounded in human positive law and in human moral philosophy, but it is not grounded in theologically-based ethics.

I feel quite certain that many of my readers will feel that I have been quite scrupulous, albeit overscrupulous, in my approach to the hunting ethic. Nonetheless, I feel that it is most important to state all possible objections to hunting from a moral perspective and examine each in order to determine whether there is merit. I have concluded that no moral objection to hunting has such merit.

For additional reading on this subject I recommend especially an excellent article by Professor Manfred O. Meitzen, "The Ethics of Hunting: A Christian Perspective" in 16 *Dialog* (Winter 1977).

Hunting and Ethics

The late Walt Disney is credited with having done that which even God did not do: he made animals human. Through Mickey Mouse, Donald Duck, and Porky Pig, Thumper and Bambi, and the Three Little Pigs, Disney gave animals all of the human characteristics with few of our faults. Americans of all ages and all walks of life came to see themselves and their neighbors in these animated little animals. We grew to love and know them as we have few humans. We created our own legends about them, and we welcomed them into our families. Children grew into adulthood, and a new generation appeared, weaned on the antics of these characters.

Disney merely popularized a notion that was well over two thousand years old when Porky Pig stammered his first line. It was a Greek slave, a hunchbacked dwarf, Aesop, who is credited with first having discovered the human characteristics of animals. A cynic and social critic, Aesop found it very convenient to criticize the first and finest persons of his day by using animal analogies. His pointed stories may not have been original with him but we have come to associate Aesop's Fables with the human-animal analogy. Legend tells that one of his stories was a bit too direct and he was cast off the mountainside (where depends on who tells the story) and killed.

The Greeks were amazed to discover that the Egyptians carried the metaphor much farther. In classical Egyptian mythology not only were certain animals sacred but the gods often had animal form. Their mythology did not find a substantial difference between men and animals. Man was merely the first among many species of animals. Mummification was practiced on animals as well as on humans. Thus, some animals might survive in the next life whereas unembalmed humans would not.

Many ancient peoples apparently believed that it was possible for humans to have intercourse with animals and to produce offspring. Only among the Hebrews, of all ancient peoples, was bestiality a crime because of a degrading difference between animals and humans. Nearly all other nations made it a crime because they feared the production of half-man, half-beast offspring. The fabled Minotaur of Crete was one such progeny of human intercourse with an animal. The gods could likewise produce children by having sexual liaison with animals, as in the case of Pan.

In more recent years a new field, bio-politics,[1] has emerged which is predicated to some degree on the extrapolation of findings about animals to human behavior. Experimental psychology studies aspects of animal behavior with the hope of applying such findings to human behavior patterns. Much medical research is done using animals as subjects, again in the hope that what is discovered can be of help to human beings.

New fields of study have probed the possibilities of communications with animals. Going far beyond the simple training of birds to repeat voice patterns, this research assumes that we might one day talk with the higher apes, dolphins, and other animals. Some believe that one can even stimulate plants by talking with them, and that cutting into plants wounds them, causing pain.

Some animal protection groups believe that animals have natural and/or legal rights.[2] Just as certain natural rights thinkers believe that man has certain inalienable rights, so also do some believe that members of the animal kingdom possess literal rights. Some protectionists claim that in an enlightened society such as the United States, animals should have the same kinds of enforceable rights that humans have. Some of these rights should now be recognized under the federal or state constitutions and under the codes of law of the United States or of the fifty states. Some claim that even if it were proven that animals presently have no such rights, it is to be expected that one day they will be afforded the protection of the law. They hold that where animals have no rights there are no true human rights either; and where animals cannot live, neither can humans live.

"Antihunting sentiment in North America, as well as in Europe, continues to proliferate at an alarming rate and has become a political force threatening the future of hunting as a sport."[3] So wrote a recent commentator on the future of hunting in America. Traditional literature on hunting has not focused on defending the sport because there was no need to do so until recently. It was simply accepted as a legitimate sport, and justifications have not been required. After all, everyone hunted.

As the anti-gun movement grew in the 1960s and into the 1970s one adjunct movement sought to limit hunting. Any use of firearms by individuals had to be evil and thus, because of the association of the two, hunting itself had to be evil. The gun was judged to be a tool of the violent and misguided elements of society. Thus, anything the individual might do with a gun must be wrong. The hunter, by association, was a misdirected gun owner.

Beyond the usual rhetoric of the anti-firearms movement, a body of literature developed which sought to attack hunting as an institution.[4] There are six principal arguments used against hunting. In summary form, these arguments may be stated as follows.

First, hunting is said to be uncivilized. Man as hunter is really primitive man, untouched or barely touched by the more civil aspects of his society. Primitive man was quite like the animals and was, himself, the ultimate predator. But he had the capability to raise himself up and to overcome this base aspect of his character. Truly civilized man would not seek to kill anything.

Second, hunting is said to be murder. The animals possess a kind of wide-eyed innocence. They would harm no one. They live in peace, harmony and tranquility until disturbed by man. They are like Bambi and Thumper in the Walt Disney movie. Then man comes and upsets the natural order of things. He slaughters the innocent for his sadistic pleasure. He brings a kind of pain unknown to the animal kingdom heretofore. How cruel indeed is man who seeks his pleasure through the pain and suffering of these innocent beings!

Third, hunting is condemned because of the possible harm that may come to man himself. Hunters kill other hunters. Hunters suffer heart attacks and injure themselves. They damage trees and fences and destroy public and private property.

Fourth, hunting produces aggression. As man becomes civilized he is supposed to reject violence. But by hunting, man acquires martial skills. He practices on animals against the day he may choose to kill other men, whether on an individiual basis or in organized, mass murder called war. Hunting sharpens his skills and gives him a taste for the taking of human lives. Hunting allows man to create fantasies of permissible hostility. Rather than suppressing and rejecting his more base appetites for violence, man transfers these violence tendencies to the field and forest. Hunting helps to keep alive these degrading sentiments. if man did not hunt he would soon overcome his tendencies to destroy any form of life.

Fifth, man is alleged to hunt only to prove his masculinity. Backed by some research on personality structures, this objection to hunting assumes that man must prove his "macho" image by killing helpless animals. The greater the kill, the greater the masculine im-

age. From the hunter's perspective it is assumed that hunting proves
that one is not a homosexual. Only "real" men hunt; unmasculine
men prefer to pursue less violent varieties of recreation. This position thus assumes that some men need to prove their own super-
male status by hunting and that such men also assume that non-
hunters are suspect in regard to their manhood. Thus, a hunter is
assumed to be more a man than his non-hunting counterpart. It is
an obvious return to primitive standards wherein the men were
hunters while the women and the weak and the old men were
gatherers, gardeners, and processers of food. By hanging the head
or other part of a dead animal on his wall, the hunter has proved by
trial his maleness.

Sixth, hunting is alleged to have an adverse effect on animal life.
This argument holds that we would still have many of the now extinct animal species had it not been for hunters; and that hunters are
responsible for nearly destroying most, if not all, of the endangered
animal species. Presumably, if all hunting ceased, then we need not
fear for our remaining animal species.

Virtually all antihunting arguments may be fitted into the six
categories provided above. Each has its own supporters, although
many members of the antihunting fraternity subscribe to all six, and
nearly all support more than one of these arguments. The conclusion suggested by each of the six arguments is that hunting is wrong
and that hunting harms both the hunted and the hunter.

Against this background it is not too surprising that some men
have concluded that hunting is indeed murder and that the killing of
animals is akin to capital punishment. The term "murder" is frequently used in descriptions of the slaughter of baby seals for their
fur or to describe the harvesting of deer, squirrels, and rabbits. If
one will admit that there is at least a reasonable analogy between the
willful taking of human life and the taking of animal life then he is
forced to admit that hunters are murderers and that hunting seasons
are but periods of legalized murder.

In discussing hunting as murder we shall make several basic
assumptions. First, we reject any analogy between the wanton killing of human beings and the harvesting of animals. Second, we
refuse to accept any notion of human-ness attributable to animals.
Third, we find no tradition within our Judaeo-Christian heritage of
this essential animal-human analogy. Fourth, while we do not
discard the findings of the students of biological evolution, we do
believe that any notion of evolution must take into account the fact

of divine intervention at that critical point at which animal life is said to have become human.

If one rejects the Biblical idea of creation, substituting for it an atheistic notion of pure evolution, he may conclude that killing of animals constitutes murder. Indeed, the animals of the world become, literally, the cousins of men. One then returns to the ancient Egyptian finding that animals and men are not substantially different. One might say only that man as the most powerful of the animals can, by right or force, take what he chooses irrespective of any relationship with the animals, and thus permit his species to hunt other animal species simply because he can do it. Such an argument is no stronger than that which would hold that man, as the highest of animals, ought to have a moral sense of obligation not to kill his brothers or his cousins.

We find that for theological reasons one must reject any notion of kindredship with the animals. In Genesis, God clearly gives man complete and unlimited dominion over the animals. We also find that this Darwinian notion of evolution does not require that one conclude that there is no substantive difference between men and the animals. Many theologians, notably Pierre Teilhard de Chardin, found reason to accept theories of evolution while retaining God and his divine intervention in the evolutionary process at the precise moment man was born of his animal ancestors.

If one merely concludes that man is the highest of the animals but not substantially different from them, he might justify his hunting of them if he was in dire need of food for survival; but he could not easily justify his hunting for sport and pleasure. If man is not substantially different from the animals, and if he did not have a moral sense wholly different from anything developed in the animal world, hunting could be viewed as the mere product of man's predatory nature and thus related to his being a meat-eater. There would be no sport hunting, for man would not be pursuing pleasure but rather impulse and instinct.

In a natural way, man is a part of the entire process of the classic balance of nature. Whole animal species have been killed off by other species, some of which were, in turn, destroyed by still other species. Man alone has the power to attempt to prevent the extermination of species. No wolf or lion, panther or hyena can establish game preserves and introduce scientific breeding methods. Man can destroy, but he can also preserve. In his quest for preservation he has undertaken the creation of a whole branch of human knowledge, game management. In its purest sense, game management seeks to maintain, propagate, control, and protect wild animals. This is not done to help man directly or as an intellectual game. It is done in the altruistic desire to maintain natural conditions and to better animal species so that they maintain themselves. Game managers seek not to produce a better and more marketable bird or animal but to strengthen, in cooperation with established laws of nature the existences of many types of animal life.

In the past, man was not generally capable of destroying whole species of animal life. He was a predator capable of killing some portion of the total harvest of some game species. As modern technology gave him increased means to destroy animals, it also provided him with the tools to protect and re-establish animal life. And, because he had a moral sense, man found ways to control the most greedy members of his kind through laws and other protections.

In modern society those who oppose hunting frequently disregard all attempts made by hunters to restore animal life through the scientific repropagation of animal species. They most frequently have found all killing of wildlife to be murder.

If one argues the basic proposition to absurdity one concludes that it is quite wrong to kill anything. The fact of life is that, in our chain of existence, something must die in order that others may live. An animal or bird is killed and consumed by another animal or bird. A plant is killed so that an animal or bird, fish, or reptile may live. It is difficult to determine what criteria are to be used in determining where the chain is to be broken. One may argue that, among animals — that is, among living beings less than man — it is permissible to kill other animals. If this harvesting of animal life is to be stopped it reduces man to vegetarian diets. If this harvesting of animal life is to be permitted in slaughterhouses and on farms exclusively, then reasoning of some substance must be developed so that one can differentiate between legitimate and illegitimate killing of animals. Presently we do not have a reasoned argument that permits us, on rational grounds, to determine why organized and commercial slaughter differs in kind from the murder of animals in the woods and in the fields by hunters.

One cannot reason that animals killed in slaughter houses are necessarily killed without pain, and that animals killed by hunters are necessarily killed with great pain. We have not as yet developed standards which say that only so much animal pain is permitted, and no more, in the harvesting of animals. We have also not yet come to the conclusion that animals raised exclusively for market are to be permitted to suffer death, albeit only slightly, whereas those animals living in nature are not to be made to suffer deaths at the hands of men.

If one is to outlaw hunting, one must then ask himself if he also intends to prevent all killing of what is ordinarily called sentient life. For example, one must decide if one may kill fish but not animals, reptiles but not birds, plants but not animals. One might also be called upon to decide which animals may be killed. One might kill rats but not rabbits; mice but not squirrels; and moles but not ground hogs.

If one wishes to carry on the reduction to absurdity he might argue that indeed fishing as well as hunting causes pain, and thus one must outlaw fishing as well as hunting. He might also argue that, as our research grows stronger and more precise, grave harm befalls plants when flowers, fruits and vegetables are plucked away from their stems and branches. The plants may be found to suffer some adverse stimulation that can be likened to pain and suffering. Surely the higher plants seem to react to stimuli in ways similar to pain reactions in lower animals.

To return more to reality, one is faced with grave difficulties in creating a meaningful dichotomy between allowable commercial killing and the killing that occurs in hunting. The simple fact is that when animals are domesticated they are tamed so that they may serve man. Only a few are tamed to be used as pets, and the remainder are prepared for eventual slaughter for meat, for hides, or for other useful parts of their bodies. Even those used for non-injurious by-products, such as eggs or milk, are destined for eventual slaughter.

We ordinarily permit killing of humans only in cases of defense of home, family, property and self, and as retribution for crimes committed against the body politic. The latter case would hardly apply to animals, and the former cases would only rarely apply. The overwhelming majority of cases in which humans are involved in the taking of animal life, excepting those killed by hunters, concern the planned killing of animals for reasons of convenience to man. Once again we arrive at the point that if the killing of animals in hunting constitutes murder, then all of us, excepting vegetarians who use no animal carcass by-products, are either guilty of murder or are accomplices in murder.

We find it impossible to conclude that the term "murder" can be applied to the killing of animals. However, this does not mean that the taking of animal life is necessarily acceptable, especially in the act of hunting. Hunting may still be rejected as a form of human activity provided we are prepared to conclude that it is degrading or dangerous to humans.

The control of hunting does not legitimately accrue to the state because animals have rights. Rather, it comes from the power of the state to act *in loco parentis,* controlling human conduct that is immoral or wrong according to that moral code that is acceptable to the society. If a man were willingly and purposefully to torture an animal, his power to do so could be countered by existing powers of the state over the acts of man. But this control would be found in the moral code of men (and their God), and written in their legal code as norms of human behavior which men might not violate.

The code of law of civilized states might proscribe actions of men who willfully inflict pain on animals. Those who would defend animals, as civilized men must, against such abuses must look to the moral and legal codes of men for help and not to abstract and unenforced natural rights of animals. The state might make willful abuse of wild and domesticated animals a crime, and it might prohibit wasteful killing of certain animals, or the wasteful killing of all animals under conditions of needless suffering. But the thrust of the law would be against wrongful human behavior and not toward protection of alleged rights of animals.

Murder is wrong because it violates the natural and legally recognized rights of those killed. In those natural rights societies, such as the United States, which follow John Locke's paradigm of human existence, each of us has a right to his life, his liberty, and his property. None of these may be taken away without due process of law. My life is one of my properties, presumably the most important of my many possessions. One who chooses of his own willful volition to take away my life has committed a crime against my property.

In traditional natural rights thinking, only man has rights and properties. Man's essence is found in his possession of civil rights and natural liberties. Man is a rights-possessing animal. This is precisely what separates him from all other animals, makes him what he is, and gives him his distinguishing characteristics. If the possession of rights is so much a part of man's being that it can be used to separate him from all other forms of being on this earth, then it is both necessary and logical to assume that no other form of being here and now possesses rights.

An animal has no right to live in any way similar to the right a man has to live. Its life is not its natural or its civil right. Life is an attribute of an animal, just as are its fur or feathers, feet or fangs. But it does not possess a natural right to live. No court made up of human beings could be expected to consider a case involving an alleged right of an animal.

Once again we must return to the hierarchy of beings in this world. The highest of known beings is man. He is qualitatively quite a different thing from the animals beneath him. He is the end of the known Creation. Other things, including animals, exist precisely because man is known to exist. They are, morally and theologically, his possessions for man was given dominion over them. In the same vein, and for the same theological reasons, they are part of the earth man is permitted to subdue.

If hunting is to be condemned one must assume that the Bible is in error, for the Old Testament speaks highly of hunting and extols the virtues of being a "mighty hunter." One of the primary functions of the Bible is to point the way to correct human behavior and to condemn the ways of evil. While many human actions are proscribed, nowhere, in the Old or the New Testament, do we find hunting condemned or repudiated as action unbecoming to men of God. Conversely, we find many of the great men of the Old Testament hunting; and Christ and several of his disciples fished. If the hunting of wild animals is murder, then many of the mighty hunters of Hebrew times were murderers, and, if, more generically, the taking of all life is murder, then Christ was either a murderer or an accomplice to murder.

The only possible rejection of this argument comes from the view that holds that moral circumstances change. Such pragmatic ethics might conclude that while hunting and/or fishing was once necessary and acceptable it is no longer the case. The peoples of earlier epochs had to hunt and fish, for they were predators. Modern man is civilized and need not rely on such misbehavior. Such arbitrary changes of moral standards are not unknown, but neither are they in general keeping with the general Western traditions.

In days when vocabularies are bent and distorted beyond rational comprehension, nearly anything can be found in print. If allegedly irresponsible actions of corporations can be called "obscene" then

one might call harvesting of game "murder." As each of us today
permits himself the luxury of creating his own ethical system, each
of us can presumably condemn as morally wrong those things which
he does not like. As the existentialist commitment allows each of us
to condemn not only for ourselves what we do not like, but also requires that we should do this for others, then a host of human activities can be altered as to their moral content. Actions previously
forbidden to men can be allowed, and those permitted can now be
forbidden.

It is easy against this relativist-pragmatic background to see how
hunting may be condemned by one or more individuals or groups. It
is wrong precisely because the person or the group so states. There is
neither need nor respect for traditional habits of the mind unless
these modes of thinking serve our own ends. There is, of course, no
refutation of such a position. One merely denies the conclusions.

Some of the antihunting literature is profoundly philosophical
and cannot be refuted in its conclusions, but only from its beginning
premises. Of these metaphysical arguments, perhaps the most
developed and systematic derives from Pierre Teilhard de Chardin
(1881-1955)[5], a French Jesuit priest whose interest was in combining
Roman Catholic thinking with Darwinian theories of evolution. The
conclusions Teilhard arrived at are neither pleasing to the Catholic
Church nor to pure evolutionists. Some even view his ideas as
undermining Christian monotheism:

Teilhard argued that the universe is becoming ever more complex
through what he termed the inexorable "law of complexification."
All of the basic materials of the universe are profoundly historical
and are necessarily one. All constituents of the cosmos from the
most basic particles to human beings have a "conscious inner face
that everywhere duplicates the material external face." Layers of
development build, one upon the other. Above the purely material
stuff of the cosmos there is the "biosphere" of living things, and, at
the apex of this pyramid, a "noosphere" of intelligent life. While
this "thinking layer" of the noosphere places man above the biosphere, he is nonetheless grounded in both the material and bio-
spherical layers of existence. He may not do harm to any of the
companion layers, that total ecological environment from which he
sprang. Such a commitment, forced upon thinking man by the
realization of the oneness of nature, disallows the bloodsport of
hunting. Man, humbled by his confrontation with nature and the
cosmos, dares not harm the less developed inhabitants of the bio-

sphere. As man moves, necessarily, toward a final oneness, termed by Teilhard the "Omega Point," he attains a hyperpersonal consciousness that precludes attacks on nature. Thus, he will neither rape the physical environment, nor hunt and kill its animal life.

Only slightly less sophisticated than Teilhard's philosophical rejection of hunting was Albert Schweitzer's.[6] A great humanitarian, author, physician, and man of letters, Schweitzer (1875-1965), developed a profound respect for nature which culminated in a complete "reverence for life" directed at all living things. Schweitzer concluded that life is the most precious gift God bestowed on creation. Its value is so great that it defies the ability of man to appreciate it wholly. That which man cannot possibly comprehend he must meekly and humbly accept. His imperfect intellect may articulate a defense of hunting and killing animals, but that argument cannot take full measure of that infinitely greater one of total respect for all life. If we could but understand how life is to be treasured and cherished, we would see how our pro-hunting arguments would fail. Since we cannot comprehend the pro-life position fully, we must defer our thoughts and sublimate our anti-life desires and appetites.

In a sense, Schweitzer made man custodian over all that lived. Because he cannot understand why he was made, such a shepherd does not invalidate the fact that he has been given, presumably by God, such a dominion. It is man's moral responsibility to see that he has been made trustee of all that lives. Just as God stands guard over us, infinitely inferior beings, so have we been given the task of safeguarding those markedly inferior beings, the animal kingdom. Man might be charged, under this general responsibility, not only with safeguarding animals from men, but protecting them from one another.

The vitalistic philosophy of Schweitzer and others, including most Indian and some other Asian philosophies, suffers from a reduction to absurdity. A physician may not kill off disease organisms, for these are a form of life. One may not kill rats that are eating food supplies, for they are living beings. One may not kill a snake that threatens a baby in a crib, for the snake is a form of life that must be protected and respected. A plant virus may not be destroyed, for it is living being.

That Schweitzer did not live by his philosophy is shown in his own admission that he kept a gun to kill snakes and wild animals that threatened him and his friends. He willingly used antibiotics to kill disease organisms and pesticides and other chemicals to protect his garden. The concluding point is noted by Schweitzer himself when he spoke of ". . . the cruel drama of the will to live divided against itself. . . ." One must then set an arbitrary dividing line to commit to action as God's custodian over living beings. It is no more arbitrary to set it beyond hunting, so as to permit hunting, than it is to set it so as to make hunting impermissible.

As one begins to move away from wholly philosophical condemnations of hunting he encounters a strange statement of the doctrine of evil. Some writers have come to view several of man's many pleasurable pursuits as evil for the sake of evil. The underlying assumption of such essays has consistently been that the taking of any form of life constitutes an evil. One may arrive at that conclusion either from traditional ethics, such as the morality of the Bible, or from a purely humanistic position. The argument centers on a definition: killing is wrong. It is not necessarily concluded from other ideas, but can be a starting point on its own. From Judaeo-Christian ethics, one can say that God mandated that willful taking of life is sin, and that God did not have to give a reason for this. From humanistic ethics, one merely says that he has concluded that killing is wrong in and of itself, again, requiring no further explanation.

Thus, the statement that "any activity which includes killing as a pleasurable end in itself is damnable" is not necessarily the logical culmination of other ideas. It may be the beginning point of an ethic, just as the Ten Commandments are not conclusions, but beginning points. If taking any life is wrong, then, logically and obviously, hunting is wrong. The hunter may indeed be he who "does evil for evil's sake." Note that no proof is given or need be given, for this is an assumption, not a conclusion that flows from evidence. Hunting is evil, and the hunter an evil-doer, only because the writer has said that it is so. This circular argument carries no more weight than one that says that hunting is a moral activity, and the hunter a doer of good things, because we think it to be so in the context of, and as a beginning point of, our philosophy of right and wrong.

If we begin somewhat earlier, assuming that the conscious desire to inflict pain is wrong, and conclude from that starting point that hunting is evil, then we need to approach the problem yet another way. Man does not, or at least should not, hunt to inflict pain, and thus derive his pleasure from the agony of the animal. Rather, he hunts to kill his prey, and in the course of hunting, may unintentionally inflict pain on his quarry. A farmer does not raise beef cattle, hogs, or chickens in order to watch them suffer at the time of the slaughter. He raises these animals to provide food, although he recognizes that, as a result unwilled and unintended pain may result to the animal.

The assumption that one hunts in order to obtain enjoyment from an animal's prolonged suffering is wholly without foundation. The writer may assume that it is so, but what the hunter truly intends may be an entirely different matter. To ascribe such a sadistic motivation to hunters generally is to entirely misread the definition of hunting.

The pseudo-scientific literature of hunting as repressed sexual activity is yet another misreading of the motivation of the hunter. There is a body of literature that asserts that man hunts either to vent his sexual frustration, or to vent his sexual drives through the sublimation of hunting. A gun becomes a phallic symbol and the animal pursued becomes the object of sexual desire. Man conquers the animal in the same way that a rapist might subdue and sexually assault a female. The kill is likened to ejaculation, and the sense of fulfillment is much like a completed sex act. These themes are interwoven in a significant portion of the antihunting literature, especially within that body of material produced by women. The hunter has been reduced to the position of being a sexually immature, unfulfilled and frustrated and probably mentally ill creature who is in need of therapeutic help.

I have not found, to date, a satisfactory explanation for female participation in the hunt expressed in such sexual terms. Either the people writing from this viewpoint are unaware of female hunters, or they are unable to account for their participation as a sexual experience and ignore them. I had rather expected to see suggestions either of repressed lesbianism or of repressed aggression — that is, that society will not permit a female to be the active and seductive sexual partner and thus hunting provides an outlet for such sublimated and frustrated feelings. I found none, because the sexually based literature concentrates wholly on the male hunter. It would seem that, logically, a sexual explanation for hunting ought to be as useful to explain female hunting as it is to explain male hunting.

Perhaps the inability of this volume of antihunting literature to articulate a satisfactory explanation for female hunters suggests a fallacy in its general approach to men as well. Further, there is no scientific literature that proves conclusively what it asserts about

repressed sexuality. The insistence on tying guns and hunting to sexuality may tell us as much about the sexual hang-ups of the authors
as it tells us about the sexual problems of hunters. Guns may, in
some cases, be phallic symbols, but so, also, may a wide variety of
other objects men and women enjoy or possess. That objects are
phallic symbols tells us nothing about their moral dimension or
healthiness. Men who hunt will admit frequently to enjoying a feeling of manliness as a result of participating in the sport. But so also
does such a feeling emanate from other human activities, certainly
including other sports. This, again, says nothing of the healthiness
or morality of the sport. It tells us nothing of the feeling of
manliness or femininity women may feel as a result of hunting. It
does not tell us whether, through the hunt, a man is escaping from
repressed homosexuality, or a women is rejecting, perhaps unconsciously, lesbianism.

Without denying that some man or some woman has hunted for
unhealthy or immoral reasons, we have no conclusive medical,
psychological or psychiatric literature that proves that, by and large,
hunting differs, as a form of human activity, from other physical
sports such as football. It is quite possible that hunting is a sport in,
of, and unto itself, even though it may also produce a feeling of
"manly" fulfillment for males. That is to say, that, although some
men may hunt precisely to feel like a man — and that is said without
an attending moral judgment — it is an accidental, secondary, and
not a major reason for hunting.

There is another argument that may seem as bizarre to a great
many of the antihunters of more conventional and philosophical
nature as it does to most hunters. It suggests that man loves war,
and, in the absence of war, he chooses to act out a fantasy of battle
in the woods. These writers frequently place a military vocabulary in
the mouths of hunters. The hunters move through the woods, apparently like a division of soldiers going into battle, ready to destroy
the enemy. The animals they seek are viewed somewhat like, if not
identical to, enemy troops.

Since the prey is an "enemy," it would seem logical that the
hunter is on a "seek and destroy mission" and that he must wholly
exterminate his victims. In a perverted society in which a degree of
immortality is accorded an assassin, one would presume that a nearly equal secular salvation could be granted to the chap who killed
the last of a species. John Doe (if you will excuse the use here of the
name of the female deer), an otherwise easily forgotten and sad little

man, has his place in the memory of mankind, whether he kills a great (or not so great) political figure, or the last elk, or mountain goat, or even rabbit or deer.

In the meanwhile, hunters are out there killing away, destroying wildlife in a wanton manner, just as warriors kill men for the sake of being able, metaphorically or really, to place a feather in their caps as proof of the kill. A deer head, a rabbit's foot or the horns of a goat are like a Congressional medal of honor, a purple heart, or a battle star. They are proof that macho man has met the enemy on the field of honor. They are living proof of his conquests.

While I admit to being very poor at fathoming the intent of much of the counter-culture and modern art expressions, my own impression of the intent of the movie, "The Deer Hunter," was that there was no difference between hunting men in war and hunting deer in the field and that the true hero (or was it anti-hero?) could move without adjustment from one to the other. As long as we have hunting, then, we shall have war, and vice-versa. The message, then, may have been that violence merely breeds on itself, and that a place to break the vicious circle of war-to-hunting-to-more war, and so on, was to end the barbarism of hunting.

If one can accept the premise that hunting and war are much the same thing, then we should have no difficulty moving on to the assumption that the ultimate war-hunt in a future society might be hunting armed human beings. A bureau, governmentally sponsored or in the private sector, might sign us up in such hunts.

In a similar vein, one can think of the great thrill of being able to hunt some long-extinct game, of being able to destroy the last member of some great species. The made-for-TV movie, "The Last Dinosaur," pitted the great hunter, played by Richard Boone, against a dinosaur that was discovered in, of all places, a hollow earth. Boone went with no intent other than to destroy the last of these great reptiles. He was justly killed in the effort, but he had gained immortality.

Again, we must return to the opening assumption. The hunt, as we have defined it and used it throughout this book, has nothing to do with causing a species to become extinct. We have assumed the contrary, that hunters want to preserve a species so that they and future generations can continue to hunt it. Hunters have, as we have shown, taken action that can only be interpreted as ones designed to ensure the continuation of those species that can be, and are worthy of being, hunted. Since man has come to control his destiny through

popular, democratic techniques and devices, he has sought to prevent the actions of single individuals who seek the strange kind of
immortality that can be gained by killing off the last of a species.
Such a thing may have been possible in an authoritarian regime, but
it is unlikely (and unpopular) in a democracy.

We have shown that skills learned in hunting may be useful in the
military. This, we admit freely, and note as being especially important as a mainline defense of the right to hunt. It does not necessarily follow that because one hunts he desires war, and it does not
follow that because one learned to kill men in war he wants to kill
animals in the field. That assumption is no more true than one that
might hold that man will become a criminal, killing other human beings at home, just because he killed men in war. It is possible, but it
does not, in either case, fit many.

One may set up empty beer cans and knock them over with an air
rifle, pretending they are enemy soldiers. A man may use a knife to
chop off corn stalks, while pretending they are the enemy and he is a
great knight. He may set up bales of hay and shoot them with a
large bore rifle, pretending they are anything his imagination may
conceive. Or he may do any of those things without acting out a fantasy. So also may man hunt with or without an accompanying fantasy. Should he act out such a fantasy, whether against insentient objects such as cans, or against sentient beings such as animals, one still
is hard-pressed to conclude that an immoral act has occurred.

The conclusion we must draw is that the argument fails precisely
because there is no proof, either of the commonality of such fantasies, or of their immoral nature. A great argument against hunting
has been built on improper and inadequate foundations.

Societies have, for many years, sought to control the activities of
men, assuming that there is some great communal right to control
what men do with their lives. One portion of the antihunting literature concentrates on the dangers of hunting to the hunters themselves. They argue that hunters shoot and kill other hunters. Some
hunters become lost and die of exposure or starvation or dehydra-
tion. Others suffer fatal heart attacks or strokes. Some fall and injure themselves. In short, they assume that because there are
dangers inherent in hunting, the great Leviathan, the state, has the
right to regulate and control this activitiy. While I presume that
some of this kind of argumentation is really based on a lie — that is,
that the proponents are more interested in stopping hunting than in

protecting hunters from themselves — let us assume for the moment that the idea is worthy of an examination.

The freedom of man, accepted by nearly every Western philosopher and theologian from Plato to the present, suggests limitation on state power. That, precisely, is what separates a democratic from a non-democratic state. If we deny man his freedom we have lowered man's nature, changed his very being and altered his fabric. He is free to choose those things which may be harmful, but that involves only a question of his relation to God and to his own individuial conscience. If we assume, only for the sake of argument that hunting is dangerous to man, this does not force the conclusion that the state has the right to stop him from hunting.

As a matter of fact, hunting and shooting sports are less dangerous than many other forms of recreation. It is safer to go hunting than it is to do many things around the home, including taking a bath.

This argument fails because of the nature of democratic thought that supports individual freedom while limiting state action.

Because of the critical nature of the objection, we have chosen to take up the question of the extinction of animal species as an entire and separate chapter. In short, hunting man, as we have consistently defined him, is not responsible for the extinction or endangerment of more than a handful of species at the most. Probably, man the sport hunter is responsible for as few as five species, and, even there, for the entire number, it fell to aristocratic-authoritarian hunters, not the more broadly based democratic hunting masses.

With each of the objections to hunting we find an appropriate response. We shall not deal at any length with some of the obvious manufactured examples. Hunters — meaning sport hunters — have not killed the whale, and they do not club baby seals. They have not sought to extinguish the last carrier pigeons. They have not sought to torture and maim for pleasure in the sufferings of animals. These cases must be considered in relation to other, perhaps defensible, perhaps indefensible topics of human activity. By the same token, I have not chosen to discuss trapping. I have personal reservations about the use of leg traps, but the case is not closed. Such activity will have to be considered by others.

Animal Rights?

> If we are ever going to do justice to the lower races, we must
> get rid of the antiquated notion of a "great gulf" fixed between
> them and mankind, and must recognize the common bond of
> humanity that unites all living beings in one universal brother-
> hood.   (*Henry S. Salt, 1892*)

In 1792 the English Neo-Platonist philosopher Thomas Taylor
wrote a book that was published anonymously under the title, *Vin-
dication of the Rights of Brutes.* While some writers have seen this
as the first attempt to establish the natural rights of animals, his
purpose was quite to the contrary. It was, in reality, a reduction to
the absurd of Mary Wollstonecraft's arguments for women's rights.
Indeed, the pamphlet may be viewed as a more general attempt to
ridicule the whole natural rights school of thought then prevalent in
England. If God had created all beings equal, Taylor argues, then it
must be, at least in the sight of God, that animals were also possessed of dignity and rights. Taylor gave no thought to his readers possibly missing the point. No right thinking man might assume that
nonhuman beings could possibly have rights. Such a term was
reserved exclusively for men, and, presumably then even, only to
the better classes.

But some men had taken these arguments for animal rights seri-
ously before Taylor's bitter sarcastic attack appeared in print.[1] Bernard de Mandeville in 1723[2] had argued that "men of any tolerable
good nature could never be reconciled to the killing of so many
animals for their daily food as the bountiful earth provides them
with varieties of vegetable dainties." The neo-gnostic argument for
the immortality of animal souls is found both in John Hildrop's
Free Thoughts upon the Brute Creation (1742) and Father
Bougeant's *Philosophical Amusement upon the Language of Beasts*
(1740). Others picked up that cry. In 1746 Robert Morris wrote his
A Reasonable Plea for the Animal Creation, arguing that "we have
no right to destroy, much less eat of anything which hath life."
Richard Dean misused Scriptural passages in his *An Essay on the
Future Life of Brutes* (1767), trying to establish that animal souls
survive their bodies.

Clergy joined in by the middle of the eighteenth century, condemning hunting and other sports wherein they alleged animals were abused. Some even claimed that one might sin against animals. James Granger's *An Apology for the Brute Creation* (1772) was a widely quoted sermon condemning cruelty to animals which suggested hellfire for those who hunted. The Reverend Doctor Humphrey Primatt suggested applying the Golden Rule to our relations with animals. Since they do not hunt us, we should return that favor. This position reminds one of Cleveland Amory's "Support your Right to Arm Bears" under which doctrine, presumably, one should give bears guns wherewith to defend themselves against rude hunters who have violated this rule.

Probably the best of the very early treatises against hunting is contained as an essay in Soame Jenyns' *Disquisitions on Several Subjects* (1782). Seven years later the distinguished British essayist-philosopher Jeremy Bentham argued for some rights for animals in his *Introduction to the Principles of Morals and Legislation* (written 1779, published 1780). He lamented that "other animals, which, on account of their interests having been neglected by the insensibility of ancient jurists, stand degraded into the class of things." He argued that since we have discovered that the color of skin has no bearing on one's human status, then, also, so should we refuse to accept as meaningful any segregation based on humanity and non-humanity within the animal kingdom. In short, animals may have some considerable standing one day in courts as beings possessed of rights.

As Western civilization became acquainted with the Eastern religions some Westerners were influenced by the Hindu and similar respect for all life above that of vegetables. John Oswald's *The Cry of Nature* (1791) did much to popularize the Indian belief that all life is sacred and that it is not permissible to kill any animal in order to eat of its flesh, or to otherwise degrade members of the animal kingdom. Indeed, the Author of Life had intended that mankind should learn to respect the basic value of all living things.

Eastern vegetarianism swept much of the West. It was rooted in Hindu mysticism and its belief in the transmigration of souls. Some earlier Western writers had suggested, possibly tongue in cheek, that animals had perhaps within them the tormented souls of sinners. Such a legacy was related to the strange teachings of the not-fully-suppressed gnostics. Reinforced by Eastern teachings, apostles of this bizarre idea promulgated the suggestion that some souls, perhaps all souls, were judged after each life, and that those whose lives had been less than exemplary had been imprisoned in animal bodies to learn of humility, charity, love and so on. Thus, transgressions against animals were truly inhuman. One who hunted might be punished, coming back as a snail or slug. In effect, the teaching about transmigration of souls led one to the conclusion that the souls of *all* beings were human, real or only potentially so. In one stroke such doctrine obliterated any possible distinction of qualitative nature between man and the animals.

By the end of the eighteenth century animal rightists had begun to view the liberation of animals in the same light as the liberation of slaves. Slavery was being abolished formally in Europe by 1800, and by mid-nineteenth century slavery had been formally outlawed everywhere in the civilized West. The abolitionist movement telescoped into the area of animal rights. Henry S. Salt's classic *Animal Rights* (1892) built on the writings of earlier writers, such as George Nicholson's *on the Conduct of Man to Inferior Animals* (1797), Thomas Young's *An Essay on Humanity to Animals* (1798), *Moral Inquiries on the Situation of Man and of Brutes* (1824), and Edward Byron Nicholson's *The Rights of An Animal* (1879).

Organizations dedicated not only to the abolition of cruelty toward animals, but to the liberation of sub-human species, grew up. Lewis Gompertz, author of the *Moral Inquiries on the Situation of Man and of Brutes* (1824) became an active secretary to the Society for the Prevention of Cruelty, and he founded the Animals' Friends Society. The Friends published a major journal which had considerable circulation and influence in Great Britain throughout the latter portion of the nineteenth century. While they were influential in stopping certain abuses of animals which were sorely in need of correction, the Friends also opposed hunting and were generally practicing vegetarians. By 1852 the Friends' journal *Animals Friends* was so influential that subscriptions permitted the publication of many of its more eloquent pieces in book form.

The work begun by Gompertz was carried further by a Belgian known as T. Forster. His book, *Philozia,* was dedicated to Gompertz and to the Animals' Friends in whose work he also engaged. The Friends rejected such milder works as the Reverend Doctor William H. Drummond's *The Rights of Animals* (1836) because the latter objected only to vivisection and accepted hunting and meat-eating.

A prominent veterinarian named Youatt argued against abuses of animal rights in *The Obligation and Extent of Humanity to Brutes* (1839). His objections to hunting and to the eating of meat were mixed in with more professional observations on animal husbandry. The book lent the authority of a physician who had dedicated his life to the protection and care of these beasts to the whole plethora of other objections toward hunting and for animal rights. A new anti-hunting audience opened up through this publication, for William Youatt was a Fellow of the Royal Veterinary College and the author of several standard textbooks on the care of animals. He argued that while human rights may be abused, they are at least recognized. However, the rights of animals are neither enforced nor generally recognized.

In 1874 the Reverend J.G. Wood published an essay, *Man and Beast Here and Hereafter,* in which he alleged that animal souls enjoy immortality. He attempted to show that the Bible did not preclude a heaven for animals. He also attempted to demonstrate that animals have been proven by the findings of modern science to share all the basic attributes of man, including reason, language, memory and a sense of moral responsibility. He claimed that animals express the full range of human emotions, notably, but not limited to, love, responsibility and unselfish behavior. Lastly, Wood claimed that, since men expected to retain their human qualities after life, it was equally reasonable to conclude that animals did likewise.

There was little novel about Wood's thesis. Indeed, three years earlier, Ezra Abbot had published a bibliography of works that held some or all of Wood's views. "The Literature of the Doctrine of a Future Life" (1871) contained over a dozen entries referring to the fact or presumption of animal immortality.

One of the most eloquent arguments against human beings eating animals was Howard Williams' *The Ethics of Diet, a Catena of Authorities Deprecatory of the Habit of Flesh-eating* (1883). It of course states the basic vegetarian thesis, adding a list of authorities who oppose the eating of animals. Its arguments from authority are well stated and the author had put some considerable effort in gathering this impressive list, although its statement of animal rights was not definitive. Like the Abbot bibliography on animal immortality, this book is most valuable as a source of opinion.

The animal rightists were not without their contemporary critics. The classic restatement of the generally acknowledged Christian position[4] is Philip Austin's *On Duty Towards Animals* (1885). This essay was written from a classic Augustinian position. He ridiculed the idea that man should show courtesy to animals. The idea of equality of being or of type he thought was insane. Man lowered himself, in direct violation of his basic religious tenets, when he assumed that things could be predicated equally of man and beast. There is no equality of type or order of being. He wrote, "it is found that an advocacy of the rights of brutes is associated with the lowest phases of morality, and that kindness to brutes is a mere work of supererogation." Medieval morality, while not ignoring the suffering of animals, nonetheless saw that it had no lasting effect as beasts perished and had no relation to ultimate suffering or final destiny. Animals were the "slaves" of mankind affording only a valuable object lesson to humanity. Austin not only accepted hunting and fishing and meat-eating, he advocated it "to demonstrate in a practical way man's dominion over the brutes."

In the same vein, Roman Catholic theologians W.E. Addis and T. Arnold, in the 1884 edition of the *Catholic Dictionary* were forced to respond to increasing allegations of animals rights. In that updating of a standard Roman Catholic reference on points of faith, doctrine, and morality, the authors deny the whole issue of rights for animals. "As the lower animals have no duties, since they are destitute of free will, without which the performance of duty is impossible, so they have no rights, for right and duty are correlative terms." The authors note further that animals are "made for man, who has the same right over them which he has over plants and stones." Man could use animals for any legitimate purpose. "He may, according to the express permission of God, given to Noe, kill them for food . . . to put them to death or to inflict pain on them." The only limitation on the use of animals is that "it is never lawful for a man to take pleasure directly in the pain given to brutes"but only because then "man degrades and brutalizes his own nature."

Other authorities have agreed with that conclusion. Indeed, it is nearly impossible to find any written work that justifies the indiscriminate injuring of animals. Bringing pain to the beasts must be justified, or man lowers his own self. As J.B. Austin, in his *The Duties and the Rights of Man* (1887) wrote, "considering that sensibility to pain is common to both men and animals, we soon perceive that to inflict needless and unjust pain . . . is to sin against one's nature, and therefore to commit a crime."

The mainstream moral view of these authors hardly made a dent in the animal rightists' arguments. Oblivious to the refutation of their points of view by standard Christian thought, they continued their struggles on behalf of their animal brethren. In 1896 the Humanitarian League of England issued its New Charter, subtitled, "a discussion of the rights of men and the rights of animals." David G. Ritchie produced his *Natural Rights* (1895) in which he argued, "we may be said to have duties of kindness towards animals." Still, Ritchie's more rational position that it "is incorrect to represent these as strictly duties towards the animals themselves, as if they had rights against us" failed to please ultra-animal rights thinkers. Henry S. Salt[5] belittled, to the satisfaction of his past and present followers, this reasonable position.

Salt and his fellow animal righters rejected any Christian argument based on difference in kind between animals and humans. As Salt wrote in response to Ritchie, "the humanitarian contention is quite clear—there is no difference in kind between man and the other animals, nor any warrant in science or ethics for drawing between them . . . an absolute line of demarcation." Indeed, Salt maintained that "if men have rights, animals also have rights in the same sense of the term." If one refuses what, to all standard Christian, Jewish, or other Western moral system, is such a basic assumption as to not require rebuttal, that is, that animals and human beings are of precisely the same ontological order, then it does follow that one must mitigate strongly for animal rights.[6]

Interest in animal rights continued under the leadership of J. Howard Moore whose *Universal Kinship* (1906) argues for three bases of the human-animal continuum of creation. Moore found that man had three links with his animal brethren on the physical, psychical, and ethical planes. On these three accounts Moore assumes that there exists a scientific basis of animal rights assertions. Moore followed the success of this work by producing *The New Ethics* (1907) which focused that science on human and animal claims to natural rights. Even without the divine guarantee of natural rights Moore concluded that there was still sufficient base for an empirically-based grant of rights to animals and humans. He assumed that a denial of animal rights on a purely pragmatic basis would also portend a denial of human rights, so tenuous is our human claim as well. Thus, pragmatically, we are compelled to guarantee animal rights out of self-protection.

Meanwhile, Henry Salt had not been idle. His leadership was reasserted in a collection of essays which he commissioned. Additional notoriety was attached to his *Killing for Sport* (1915) because of the strong endorsement of its theses by the noted author, George Bernard Shaw. The latter wrote an introduction that opened new doors to Salt's animal rightists, most notably among the intellectuals of the leftist Fabian Society. They had long held an intellectual, if not practical interest in guarantees of new freedom to the English working class. Now, a new cause had been attached, and Salt was quick to exploit this opportunity to tie animal to human rights advancement with the influential and wealthy Fabian group.

The Humanitarian League had developed some interest in literary matters, publishing several anthologies of poetry whose aim was to popularize the cause of animal rights.[7] Salt edited *Kith and Kin: Poems of Animal Life* (1901) and *The Great Kinship* (1921), both containing animal rights poetry. Among other writers to popularize the notion of animal kingdoms with human attributes were Rudyard Kipling and H. Rider Haggard. Of course, Lewis Carroll's adventures of Alice allowed for considerable discourse between animals and humans.

The fiction and aesthetics of the antihunting, pro-animal rights groups continues to this day. One can credit Walt Disney with having done that which God did not do—he made animals talk. Surely, the movies of the human-animals contributes to our present evaluation of animal rights. Many other artistic creations have gone much farther than Disney, not by trying to make animals human, but by trying to make animals into super-beings who think in modes different from, but very similar to, humans. Richard Adams's novels are especially effective in this regard. His *The Plague Dogs* (1978) attempts to show the feelings, emotions and thoughts of two canines who escape from a laboratory in which animals are used as subjects of scientific experiments. His *Watership Down* (1972), also offered as an animated cartoon moving picture, shows the world through the eyes of a rabbit. One can sense and perceive the environment only as the animal. The rabbits have a society, government, and morality as best suits their species. One shares in the triumphs and tragedies of the rabbit hero. Adams's work is qualitatively different from George Orwell's *Animal Farm* in that in the latter work one knows that animals are really human substitutes in the same sense that Aesop or Disney used them. Here, the animals are really animals, and it is their world, not the human world, that is accommodated.

Brigid Brophy's *Hackenfeller's Ape* (1968) is less effective, for the emphasis is on a scientist who merely opposes the use of animals in any kind of experiment. He applies his principles by saving an ape from being sent into space in a rocket. Francis E. Clarke provided an excellent anthology of antihunting, pro-animal rights poetry in *Poetry's Plea for Animals: An Anthology of Justice and Mercy for Our Kindred in Fur and Feather* (1927). here again the emphasis is on the human being's obligation to his brethren. More like Adams's writing is William Kotzwinkle's *Doctor Rat* (1976). This novel concentrates on the wretched life of a rat in an experimental laboratory. Margaret Tuttle's *The Crimson Cage* (1978) concentrates on the excesses of experimenters. Few human dealings with animals, especially those allegedly regulated by the government, escape her anger.

When one begins to consider modern literature that opposes hunting and asserts animal rights one hardly knows where to begin. The themes are very little different from the earlier writings. Generally, such nonfiction relies on the now-standard themes we have already explored, namely, that animals and humans are inseparably linked, that any abridgement of animal rights places man himself in jeopardy, and that God intended that animals have specific natural rights just like man's. Many defend the vegetarian life as the only acceptable path for man to travel. I have not found a single unplowed field in the current literature, proving that, as in most areas of human endeavor, there is little new under the sun. Many of the present crop of writings are inferior to the first writings in style, organization, coherence, and logic. I will admit one prejudice by way of an observation: modern literature at times seems to me to lower both man and animals as frequently as it uplifts both, and some of our contemporary writers seem willing to give animals a moral superiority to man.

One division of modern literature argues against the use of animals in scientific experimentation. In general, the authors conclude that, even if it were to be proven beyond a shadow of doubt that human lives are saved or prolonged by such experiments, these experiments are illegal, immoral, and degrading to all of creation. The National Anti-Vivisection League has sponsored two major works by M. Beddow Bayly, *Spotlights on Vivisection* (1946) and *More Spotlights on Vivisection* (1960). The same society also published Bayly's *The Futility of Experiments on Animals* (1954), the underlying premise of which—that experiments on animals are unproductive—runs counter to the findings of modern science. It seems rather basic that scientific groups would not bother to buy, raise, or keep animals just to torture them without reason. The evidence, of course, is that experiments on animals are ordinarily quite useful, althought not in every case. The same premise underlies Jeff Diner's *Physical and Mental Suffering of Experimental Animals* (1978). Diner's book offers an excellent bibliography on its subject. Perhaps the spiritual grandfather of the antiexperimentalists is Edward Evans whose *The Criminal Prosecution and Capital Punishment of Animals* (1906) objects to the killing of animals generally. Dallas Pratt's *Painful Experiments on Animals — And the Alternatives* is still in manuscript form at this writing, but at least one authority suggests that it promises a reasonable discussion of the issue. One of those who believes that experiments in laboratories do more harm than good is Hans Ruesch. His *Slaughter of the Innocent* (1978) is both a history and a critique of the medical use of animals. Much the same thesis appears in Richard Ryder's *Victims of Science* (1975). Probably the most eloquent statement came from Salt's friend and the popularizer of many of Salt's ideas, G.B. Shaw. G.H. Bowker has edited *Shaw on Vivisection* out of a miscellany of his writings. John Vyvyan has produced two major anti-experimental works, *In Pity and Anger: A Study of the Use of Animals in Science* (1969) and *The Dark Face of Science* (1971), which argue against such a misuse of animals and such an abuse of their rights.

A second objection to hunting and to virtually any relationship with animals beyond observing, feeding, or communicating with them is found in the continuing literature of the vegetarians. There is a plethora of books on the subject, many sponsored by organizations such as Theosophical Society. Nathaniel Altman's *Eating for Life* (1977) was published by the Theosophists' publishing house. Another contemporary statement of the vegetarian objection is to be found in Dudley Giehl's *Vegetarianism: A Way of Life* (1979). Henry Salt produced one of the earlier works for the Vegetarian Society, *The Logic Of Vegetarianism* (1933). One additional vegetarian statement deserves attention. Jon Wynne-Tyson is one of the more logical, eloquent, and published vegetarians. His *Food for a Future: The Ecological Priority of a Human Diet* (1975) ties the vegetarian consideration to the more general environmental-ecological arguments as voiced by the extreme elements of these movements.

Kindred studies have been written in recent years which object to
the raising of animals under "unnatural" conditions. Peter Batten's
*Living Trophies: A Shocking Look at the Conditions in America's
Zoos* (1976)[8] found much to object to in our zoological parks. But
most writers in this category have concentrated their efforts on the
farms that raise animals for meat, animal products, hides, fur, and
so on. Ruth Harrison's *Animal Machines: The New Factory Farming Industry* (1964), James Mason and Peter Singer's *Animal Factories* (1980), and Victor B. Scheffner's *A Voice for Wildlife* (1974)
all object to the raising of animals in and under controlled circumstances for efficient production. *The Brambell Report,*[9] an official
British governmental study, again arrived at somewhat negative
conclusions about intensive and efficient systems of animal husbandry. Monica Hutchings and Mavis Caver in *Man's Dominion: Our
Violation of the Animal World* (1970) fabricated a sexist attack on
man's misuse and abuse of his animal relatives. They object, in fact,
to such a range of abuses that it is difficult even to begin to chroni-
cle these crimes. Undrlying all of these studies is the omnipresent
assumption that animals have rights equal to, or nearly equal to,
those possessed by human beings. The shutting up of an animal in
an unnatural (read: domesticated) setting is the moral equivalent of
imprisoning a human being. The animals of course have been
locked away without due process of the law, held incommunicado,
and deprived of even rudimentary rights to life, liberty, and hap-
piness.

Among the many breaches of animals rights we can consider here
are these. Zoos are immoral, for they create a prison condition. Bull
fights are evil, for the bull is tortured and then killed without trial.
Capturing animals to be held as pets is a new form of slavery. No
person owns an animal, especially one which was born free. Rodeos
are nearly as evil as bull fights, for the animals may be injured without their consent. Factory production systems create, for the lack of
a better expression, deanimalized animals, animals which exist without spirit or personal reason for existence. Animals must exist in
natural surroundings to be truly animals.

John Locke had suggested, in invoking human rights liberally for
all men, that man can be human only if he can exercise his freedom
fully. As a rights-possessing animal by definition, his essence would
be prostituted if he did not enjoy his rights as Nature (Nature's
God) intended. Animals, likewise, are born free, but as Rousseau
once said of man, they are everywhere in chains. The animal right-

ists would invoke natural rights as much for animals as Locke did for man. Anything that inhibits animals from being free—that is, fully animals—changes and alters their nature, thereby making them less than true, natural, animals. Their essence, their very being, has been altered.

The natural conclusion from the aforesaid is that a new liberation ideology, perhaps theology, is mandated for the animal kingdom. There are many such books. One even contains the language of liberation in its title, *Towards a New Eden: Animal Rights and Human Liberation* (1979) by Michael W. Fox. Books that suggest the concept of animal rights are almost common. A partial listing would include: Patricia Curtis, *Animal Rights* (1980); Cleveland Amory, *Man Kind? Our Incredible War on Wildlife* (1974); James Dewar, *The Rape of Noah's Ark* (1969); Thomas Field-Fisher, *Animals and the Law* (1964) ; Andrew Linzey, *Animal Rights: A Christian Assessment .of Man's Treatment of Animals* (1976); Richard K. Morris and others, *On the Fifth Day: Animal Rights and Human Ethics* (1978); Tom Regan and others, *Animal Rights and Human Obligations* (1976); Richard Ryder and others, *Animals' Rights: A Symposium* (1979); Peter Singer, *Animal Liberation: A New Ethics for Our Treatment of Animals* (1975 , 1977); and Lewis Regenstein, *The Politics of Extinction* (1975).

One of the best known of these books is Victor Scheffner's *A Voice for Wildlife* (1974). He argues that hunting for any reason is morally wrong. The taking of seals, whales, and similar animals, especially where it threatens a species, is tantamount to a felony. While opposing killing for subsistence, Scheffner finds this less offensive than mere pleasure or market hunting. No real distinction on a moral level is made here between the sport hunter and the market hunter, although we have found this distinction both useful and real elsewhere in this book. The approach is typical for literature of this general type. Its arguments are hardly different from Amory or Regenstein and a host of others included in the animal rights literature above. There are books, of course, which attack hunting exclusively or primarily. In some cases the authors are willing to eat meat provided it is killed humanely, as in a slaughterhouse. In other cases, the authors are vegetarians; and in still other cases the authors defend any killing that is primarily done for meat, for personal or family consumption, but object to sport hunting with its alleged attendant cruelty and sadism.

In addition to the arguments included in books discussed under other topics above, we have a significant number of antihunting books. Ernest Martin's *The Case Against Hunting* is among the first of the truly contemporary sources of antihunting arguments. I suspect that this 1959 study has been read and plagerized (or nearly so) by a number of others. Patrick Moore edited a reasonably well-reasoned and straightforward essay in *Against Hunting* (1965). Probably Regenstein and Amory are the two best known anti-hunters, and sales of their books seem to justify this conclusion. While many of the animal rights antihunting books appear out of nowhere and from presses which seem to be otherwise unknown, Amory and Regenstein have made inroads with the major presses that others could not make.

Increasingly, scholars have come to the conclusion that the smoke that emanates from the antihunters' fires warrants investigation to see what, if any, fire there is. Philosophers have begun to inquire into areas such as animal rights. New books will offer more philosophical justification for both sides without solving the problem. Scholarly works, such as (at this writing) R.G. Frey's forthcoming *Interests and Rights: The Case Against Animals* will be published by academic presses which, heretofore, would have ignored the topic wholly, disdaining to consider such an unworthy subject for one of their prestigious wares.

As a personal commentary, I would like to offer certain overviews of the contemporary literature which has come from the penmanship of the majority of the antihunters. First, it seems to me that they miss the quintessential point that hunters can be separated from that group that kills only for profit, not sport. I have tried in this work to separate the whale killers, armed with high-speed ships and modern cannons, on the one hand, from the deer stalkers on the other hand. If this distinction is not made our language will have been rendered meaningless. When the remaining rebel soldiers of General Marshall Doctor Idi Amin Dada slaughter elephants with machine guns and anti-tank weapons to sell the ivory, they are not hunting. Neither are the "bunny busters" chronicled by Amory, who kill rabbits with clubs in a North Carolina "bunny bop" hunt.[10] The slaughter of young seals in Canada may be defensible, but, again, not as hunting.

By refusing to differentiate between a number of slaughtering activities and true hunting these writers have muddied the water and obscured the true issue. In my judgment it weakens any case they may have against sport hunting. In short, I cannot see that indiscriminate slaughter is the subject of either this book or of their books, if they mean to consider hunting. It is necessary to begin here with a rational distinction.

Second, the emotional appeals ignore the true issues. It may be of some interest that Amory has suggested supporting one's right to arm bears, but the proposition is clearly absurd. This Amory readily admits. Nonetheless, much of the antihunting literature subsists on such rhetoric.

The meaning and impact of animal pain has been discussed so frequently, far beyond the hunting issue, that it has warranted an entry in most dictionaries and encyclopedias of philosophy. Even if animals were not hunted, they would still experience pain. One has only to offer a few counter examples from nature. A big horn sheep falls and breaks a leg while traversing a rocky path in its native habitat. A rabbit escapes a predator, but loses a leg and goes off to die a painful death. Two buck deer interlock antlers and die of starvation. There is no interjection of human agents here. The pain is still real. There is no answer in any of these cases to questions of why the pain must be suffered. The ethical philosophers have failed to provide a reasonable explanation, just as they have failed to explain the rationale for the pain of innocent children.

Third, it would seem unlikely that an accord could be reached within the animal kingdom that would make herbivores of all species. So long as even one species preys upon another, the charge of cannibalism against meat-eating men fails. I am not certain how such a charge can be levelled against a man who must eat an animal to survive. Hypothetically, if a man is stranded without food he may not kill another man. However, most ethics would allow a man to kill a fish or bird or animal to survive. If the eating of flesh is allowed in this case, presumably it means that it is really not cannibalistic to eat meat. The discussion must then center on two points: when may I eat meat, and how may I kill the animal?

In summary I have a distinct feeling that one can become too rationalistic in responding to the antihunters. Perhaps, if one simply accepts traditional Judaeo-Christian ethics he can dismiss the whole antihunting, animal rights argument. It just does not hold in light of the necessary ontology established by this Western moral system.

The Right to Hunt and National Defense

In addition to the legal arguments for the right to hunt based wholly on court opinions there is a strong secondary argument that can be constructed on the values of hunting in the development of a strong national defense capability. In the simplest terms, the argument holds that the hunting experience helps to prepare a young person to act effectively in military training and in combat. In connection with the right to keep and bear arms, the Supreme Court of the United States has held that legal exercises designed to prepare the nation's youth for combat are at the heart of the true meaning of the Second Amendment. Accordingly, if the right to hunt can be conclusively shown to be of value in the premilitary induction preparation of our youth, such an exercise might be constitutionally protected for that, if no other, reason.

We begin our discussion with certain basic assumptions. We assume that a nation has an inherent and legal right to defend itself. We assume that a future war is conceivable. We assume that the nation may one day become engaged in a just war. A literal reading of the Book of Revelations assumes at least one future war, the Battle of Armageddon. Lastly, we assume that the best way to prevent future war in a realistic sense is to be prepared for war. It is therefore incumbent upon a nation to take every possible step to increase its defensive capability, and that includes the preparation and training of a preinduction pool of trained manpower. Such a reservoir would be comprised of citizen soldiers, persons who are engaged in other professions by vocation, and in the military only by avocation. This group would already possess certain basic military skills before being called up for service.

There is a very large number of ways a young person might prepare himself under the general umbrella of preinduction training. He might learn mountain climbing, parachuting, hiking, and survival skills. He might practice physical fitness regimens. He might keep himself fit by establishing certain dietary habits. And he might learn hunting and shooting skills that might later serve him in combat.

The state, for its part, might use its vast resources to support such training. It might provide instruction. It might offer outlets for the various activities, such as by opening up public lands for practice. It might offer monetary supports for equipment. In short, it might use a tiny, almost untracable, amount of its defense outlay to encourage the young to develop, essentially on their own para- or quasi-military skills.

In order to justify state support it would be incumbent on someone to prove that preinduction physical training is valuable to the armed forces. Such studies might be financed by grants from private sources, such as foundations, or they might be financed by government monies. The prime requisite would be that such a study be conducted by a prestigious and reputable consultant. If the realiability factor is predetermined, or otherwise established to the reasonable satisfaction of government, it would seem that government might be compelled to make a commitment to carry out the appropriate public policy.

With regard to hunting skills as preinduction training, we have such a report. It meets our basic criteria for soundness, reliability, prestige, and integrity. Indeed, the report was undertaken precisely to explore the efficacy of civilian marksmanship and hunting programs as they relate to national defense.

The Arthur D. Little Report to the United States Army is dated January 1966. Its genesis is intriguing. In the early to mid-1960s the Department of Defense sought ways to economize. One assumption was that certain programs were obsolescent or obsolete. These programs could be eliminated without jeopardizing our defensive capability.

Defense Secretary Robert McNamara assumed that the civilian marksmanship training programs could be eliminated. The two affected agencies were the National Board to Promote Rifle Practice (NBPRP) and the Director of Civilian Marksmanship (DCM). The civilian secretariat of the Army assumed that NBPRP could not stand up under close scrutiny. The original suggestion that McNamara's staff conduct an in-house study was dismissed; it was assumed that it would be self-serving.

Mr. H.J. Fitch, Acting Assistant Secretary of the Army for Financial Management allocated $100,000 for a consultant's study of NBPRP. The Army liaison officer was Colonel Louis J. North, a staff officer in the Office of the Assistant Chief of Staff for Force Development (OACSFOR). North was an experienced combat officer, a member of the Army Rifle Team, a Distinguished Marksman, and a coach of the Army international Team. He received six competitive bids, and chose the prospectus offered by the Arthur D. Little firm. North wanted the Little consultants to complete the study, not only because of the excellent reputation of the firm, but also because its chief executive officer was retired Army General James Gavin, former Deputy Chief of Staff for Operations (DCSOPS).

The Little Report was delivered in six months on a budget reduced from its original estimate of $125,000 to the $100,000 North had available. Although the six-month period is relatively short by normal governmental standards, the work was an excellent one. It consisted of 448 pages of text and 14 pages of introductory materials. Five complete copies were delivered. One went to the Pentagon library, one to the Defense Documentation Center, another to DCM, and the other two possibly ended up on the Secretary of Defense's desk. Chapters I and II of the study were mere summaries of the remaining portions, and some fifty or so copies of that document were circulated. The National Rifle Association reprinted a limited number of copies as well. The impact of these 57 pages should have been significant, but it was not.

The Little Report fell stillborn from the pens of the Army's consultants. Few writers know of its existence; fewer still have ever seen a complete copy of the report. None of its major, and few of its minor, policy recommendations were ever implemented. Although it supported retention of the civilian marksmanship training programs, support has been substantially reduced. The DCM budget is all but non-existent today. Few programs have been implemented to encourage the private sector to develop civilian marksmanship training.

Our work here concerns hunting, and it is to this point we must return. Our premise is that hunting is a vital part of a total program of civilian premilitary training and preinduction preparation. It is not a sport practiced in a vacuum. Rather, it is very much tied to the whole of shooting sports. In short, one logical culmination of riflepersonship is hunting. One can, of course, consider shooting as a thing in itself, a finality. One can also assume that one learns to shoot in order to shoot something other than paper targets. In the military one may have to shoot an enemy soldier. In civilian life he may choose to shoot an animal.

The Little Report concluded that shooters make better inductees than non-shooters. They learn to use their weapons more rapidly. They already know something of the names of parts of guns, so they pick up the Army's terms quickly. They probably already know how to clean and fieldstrip a hunting or sporting rifle, so they learn to do these things with the Army's weapon in short order. Since they already know how to shoot a gun, they learn early and well how to shoot the Army's rifle. They have some knowledge of positioning and related skills, so they begin with a head start. They are generally accustomed to the recoil of a gun, so are rarely gun shy. In short, the Little Report concluded precisely what common sense would tell the shooter about the subjects we have discussed.

Hunters enjoyed other distinct advantages. They were accustomed to carrying their guns safely, and they knew how to raise and aim (or point, as with a shotgun) their weapons in order to catch a quick shot at game. Hunters learned how to stalk game and to move quietly through the woods. They had killed moving, living objects before, and not merely shot at paper targets. They had developed a sharpened sense of awareness of other living beings in the woods, and this more basic instinct served hunters well in combat. Often, they had hiked long distances over very difficult terrain. Many had had experience in a variety of natural conditions, ranging from deserts to meadows, to snow and ice-covered ground. They had survived for periods of time under a wide variety of conditions. Most had learned certain tricks to reduce their need for regular meals or their dependency on water.

The Little Report found a number of interesting, adjunct facts about hunting and shooting. The term "shooting and hunting fraternity" is used ccommonly by sportsmen to describe themselves. The report noted few, if any, instances of bigotry and prejudice among these groups. Instead, it found that these persons were quite likely to share experiences and knowledge freely, without regard to race, religion, and national origin. They had, indeed, established a fraternal relationship among themselves. This sentiment could be likened to a comradeship in arms established among soldiers in combat situations.

Beyond its sociological findings, the Little report concluded that firearms were handled and stored safely. No instances of the abuse or misuse of guns owned or shared among the shooters or hunters could be pinpointed. No violent crimes were committed with these stores of weapons. The experts concluded that security was generally well-maintained. Safety practices were firmly established, and hunters and shooters insisted on safe procedures on the range or in the field. The unspoken assumption one can draw from the report is that safety violations, along with the resulting and accompanying accidents, might result more frequently from untrained and unorganized hunters.

The object of the military in combat situations must be to place in the field foot soldiers who will fire their weapons, thus inflicting casualties on the enemy, while avoiding, insofar as possible, injuries from enemy troops. The soldiers who had received previous firearms instructions, or who had hunted, were, according to the Little Report, more likely to use their weapons in combat than non-hunters and previously untrained individuals. They also suffered statistically significantly fewer battle casualties than their inexperienced counterparts.

The Little Report provides the hunter with solid statistical evidence that hunting and firearms training is of great value to the military. More importantly, it provides conclusive evidence that the volunteer or the conscript will be more likely to function as a soldier and survive if he has been a hunter and a shooter in civilian life. While the values that may accrue to the state are important to it and to its effectiveness as a protector of the peace, within a free and democratic society our greater concern must be for the individual.

One cannot, one should not, require an individual to wear a seatbelt by compulsion of law in a truly free, liberal society. One is likewise compelled to conclude that the state lacks the coercive power to prohibit one from smoking cigarettes despite the apparent tie between smoking and lung cancer and other illnesses. Still, the moral argument is omnipresent that, if one truly wishes to protect his health and safety perhaps he should wear his seatbelts and avoid cigarettes. By the same token, the citizen soldier, who may be conscripted or who may volunteer at any time for military service may feel impelled to choose to learn hunting and shooting skills, if for no other reason than his own survival in a combat situation. If, in the meantime, he is not required to use skills so acquired, he may derive other pleasures from hunting. The central point will have been missed if we do not stress that the obligation is entirely on the level of moral persuasion, and not on the level of legal requirement. I am not arguing here that an involuntary system of paramilitary or quasi-military training be required of each citizen, as is the case with the Voluntary Society for the Assistance of the Army, Navy and Air Force (DOSAAF) in the Soviet Union.

The Little Report merely shows us, if we choose to read it and accept its conclusion, that there is a clear tie between trainability and survival in combat and the hunting and shooting sports. One could choose to participate in other sports and training programs that would have certain applications in combat. One could learn parachuting, camping and survival techniques, or go hiking or running. Still, these are more remote from the military preparation than hunting and shooting.

If the conclusions of the Little Report are incorrect, that the hunting and shooting sports are not valuable in preinduction training, it then follows that one must attempt to disprove the theses of the report. Another study, carried on by an equally prestigious and skillful and qualified consultant must attempt to dislodge our conclusions. Such a study as a counter-example has not appeared to date. It is most unlikely that such a study will appear in the near future. Until that day when the Little Report is discredited, it would seem that the prudent individual would do well to heed its recommendations, and to follow the appropriate policy courses, on both individual and governmental levels. These conclusions command only insofar as knowledge commands over ignorance and uninformed opinion.

If the conclusions of the Little Report are correct, it should be relatively easy to find examples in which the trained hunter-shooter has excelled in combat precisely because of these skills. This is the case here. We find several famous examples. In World War I there is the case of Sergeant Alvin York, an Appalachian hunter whose hunting skills enabled him to capture or kill a significant number of German troops. In World War II there is the example of Private Audie Murphy who used his hunting skills to great advantage in both Italy and France against Nazi troops. In Vietnam American snipers and sharpshooters were recruited primarily from among the ranks of superior competitive shooters and hunters.

In Harrison Salisbury's story of the siege at Stalingrad in the Second World War he tells of the competition between two hunters operating as sharpshooters. Finally, the Soviet sniper killed his German counterpart, but only after the German had killed over 100 members of the Red Army. The German soldier had learned his trade as a hunter in the Black Forest, and the Russian had learned his as a hunter in Siberia.

There are, of course, many counter-examples of shooters who excelled in war despite having had no prior hunting or shooting experience. One can speculate on two things. They might have made, or perhaps, later, did make excellent hunters. They might have learned the skills of an excellent marksman earlier had they been shooters and hunters earlier in life.

In the final analysis, both common sense judgment and the Little Report lead us to the conclusion that hunting and shooting skills are very much integrated with the creation of a reservoir of trained manpower which is useful in an armed force. This preinduction training enables the armed force to operate more efficiently, especially during the difficult days of postinduction training; and it provides a measure of security and a margin of safety to the citizen soldier in combat.

The conclusions are simple. If America chooses to provide a margin of protection through military strength it must count, in its total strength, the preparedness of its people to serve in the armed forces. In assessing the total military power it must determine the extent to which its civilian population — the soldiers whose interests in military affairs are by avocation only — is able to be inducted into the armed forces quickly.

Funding for NBPRP and DCM must be increased. Programming aimed at city-dwellers, minorities, and the poor should be developed. Hunting and shooting programs, working perhaps through private organizations such as the National Rifle Association, or the National Shooting Sports Foundation, could be offered to those who are interested. The cost, especially when compared with the overall national defense budget, would be quite small. The benefits could be enormous.

If it is true that aversion to guns is based on ignorance, then an educational program seems to be a logical way to approach the problem. An educational program need not be dependent on the private ownership of firearms, since the NBPRP-DCM programming was based on a lend-lease principle. Owning a gun could be voluntary, not mandatory.

I suspect that the objections to such a program are based primarily on a general prejudice against guns and a specific objection to an educated and armed population. I also suspect that there are many politicians who simply distrust the masses generally and wish to control them by over-regulation. Arguments, then, no matter how well grounded in fact and statistically-based proof, will fall on deaf ears because they cannot counter a general prejudice against hunting and firearms.

The Legal Right to Hunt

The right to control the hunting of wild game has long resided with the state.[1] The state itself cannot and does not own wild animals, but it has the police power to control sport, commercial, and other hunting and killing of wild game animals, including fish and birds. Early in man's recorded history this meant a right or power to reserve game for the use of kings and nobility. As democratic ideals spread, hunting rights also were popularized. At about the same time, man learned to manage and protect game species; he developed the science of wildlife management required to assist the state in protecting these scarce and precious resources.

The courts have long made a common sense distinction between those animals that exist in the wild state and those which have been domesticated. In a free economy, the domesticated animals are free of restrictions commonly associated with hunting. The slaughter of domesticated animals is ordinarily not under those police authorities that offer oversight in the field. Subject to a few rules and regulations associated primarily with the health of the community, farmers and others may freely kill domesticated species. The courts have had remarkably little trouble distinguishing between those animals ordinarily domesticated and those which exist primarily in the wild state. Even when a species, such as foxes, is raised domestically and hunted as a sport, or for a profit, the courts have made reasonable inferences and distinctions.

Under the American federal system of shared, delegated, reserved and prohibited powers, the power to regulate the hunt has generally been considered to be a power reserved by and to the states. In an unusual case,[2] the federal courts found that this reserved power can be altered to become a shared or concurrent power as a result of a treaty arrangement. The United States Supreme Court had invalidated the first attempt by the Congress to regulate the hunting of migratory birds, holding such power to reside exclusively with the states. A subsequent treaty with Great Britain on behalf of Canada and the United States obligated the federal government to regulate the hunting of migratory waterfowl. This time the United States Supreme Court allowed the federal regulations to stand because the

133

treaty upgraded and added to federal powers as the latest expression of the American people. The case suggests not only that federal powers in policing hunting might one day be expanded again, but that federal powers vis-a-vis the states in many other areas might be extended. Thus, the regulation of waterfowl hunting presently rests jointly with the federal government and the states. Hunters are subject to both levels of government in rules and regulations and licensing.

The Supreme Court decided in 1920 that treaties may expand federal powers, allowing these powers to supersede and encroach on state prerogatives. Still, in the sixty years since this decision was rendered the federal government has not expanded into other areas of hunting regulation. Some expect that such powers, expanding from the migratory bird acts, may be used to control a wide variety of other types of hunting, including eventually all endangered species.

In areas under federal control the United States government exercises primary control. The "Alaska Lands Bill" of 1980 has expanded federal control over about nine-tenths of that state's lands. National parks, federal hunting and wildlife preserves, and federally owned primitive-wilderness and forest areas provide the federal government with a considerable quantity of land in which its authority to control, even prohibit, hunting is substantial and final. Federal land control provides us with an example of frequent over-regulation, mismanagement, and administrative boondoggle. Conflicting opinions and policies about hunting and game management have had a negative effect on hunting.

One case in point involved the endangerment of native species by artificially induced wild animals whose ancestors were once domesticated. In the Grand Canyon area under federal control, wild burros, descendants of domesticated beasts of burden, threaten native flora and fauna, but the federal government has not been able to make the hard decision to kill the new species. As we have noted earlier, governments have frequently failed to make the difficult decisions necesary to save animal species from extinction.

The federal government has frequently closed public lands to hunting. Areas acquired with tax monies are closed indefinitely for reasons that are reduced to little more than sympathy to non-hunters. Tax monies are then employed to hire professional killers to exterminate the game surpluses, leaving the carcasses to rot in the woods.

State power to control hunting is also limited in the case of those Amerindian tribes which have a treaty relationship with the federal government.[3] Some tribes retained the right to hunt on their ancestral or treaty lands.[4] Some delegated to a limited extent the right to control hunting to the federal government, but not to the states. In a few cases, treaties may permit the federal and state governments to control hunting. In the case of treaty rights, it appears that, for the most part, tribes may not permit non-Amerindians to hunt in a way that would be contrary to state law. However, tribes may prevent non-members from hunting on their lands.

States generally control most hunting.[5] States may make distinctions between their citizens and both non-residents[6] and aliens. Thus, a state may choose to reserve hunting rights to one, some, or all species to in-state hunters.[7] They may prohibit aliens from hunting at all.[8] They may set fees for hunting at rates that discriminate against out-of-state or alien hunters. They may also distinguish between residents and non-residents in bag limits.

States may set reasonable hunting seasons and they may close some seasons on species all together.[9] They may set daily and seasonal limits on kills. They may limit hunting procedures and practices.[10] They may limit weapons types and disallow weapons with certain capabilities, such as full or semiautomatic mechanisms. States may outlaw rifles or shotguns totally or for the pursuit of certain species.[11] Special seasons for certain types or levels of weapons technologies may be set aside.

States generally allow landowners to determine who may hunt on land and who may not hunt, provided the hunt is conducted within general state limitations on hunting and bag limits.[12] A landowner can ordinarily prohibit hunting generally by posting his land.[13] He may prohibit only certain types of hunting, such as the hunting of does in a state's antlerless deer season, again by posting his land.[14] States may encourage the opening of private lands by a series of enticements such as state grants and subsidies, but participation must be voluntary.

States have frequently permitted farmers to reclaim certain wild animals,[15] usually fur-bearers, and to use them much as they use domesticated animals. Thus, the landowner who has captured and enclosed game animals, treating them as domesticated beasts, may kill one or more of them[16] as is normal and common under general considerations of animal husbandry.[17]

This does not mean that an individual land-owner may kill animals at his will and pleasure. The American state courts differ here substantially from the English common law holdings. Except during the period following the Norman Conquest, when the king contended that he was lord paramount of the field and thus possessed of the right to take game exclusively, or as sovereign of the fields to grant such a right to others, landowners could ordinarily kill and use game as they chose. The courts have held that, while states cannot systematically deprive landowners of their rights to hunt wild animals, there is no vested property right to hunt irrespective of seasons or game limits.[18]

The Old English[19] term for wild animals was *"ferrae naturae"* which is meant to convey the idea that these beasts "are only such as to be reclaimed and made tame by art, industry or education and confined in order to be within the immediate power of the owner."[20] The title to such beings "is held in trust by the state in its sovereign capacity for all its citizens." The state "may protect the species from extinction by exhaustive methods"[21] of wildlife management and propagation. Fish, birds, and many mammals "are classified in the law, largely, perhaps, because of their migratory characteristics and want of fixed habitat as animals *ferrae naturae.*"[22] Animals such as "cattle are domestic animals whose possessors have the obligation to control them."[23] The domesticated animals are clearly distinguished from wild ones because *"ferrae naturae* animals are wild by nature and disposition, as opposed to *domitae naturae* which are tame animals by nature."[24] Animals which exist *ferrae naturae* "while in a state of freedom their ownership, so far as a right of property can be asserted, is in the state, not as proprietor, but in its sovereign capacity for the benefit of, and in trust for, its people in common, and they cannot be captured by anyone without express or implied permission of the state."[25]

The designation of animals is most important, for "animals *ferrae naturae,* such as deer, ducks, pheasants and swans are denominated game."[26] Again, "the word game includes beats, fowls, fish and other such animals as exist naturally in the wild."[27] For the most part, game animals are those subject to capture and pursuit as opposed to those which have no sporting value. Quoting from sources of English and American common law, the courts have generally agreed that game animals are animals which may be or even should be hunted. Thus, "game means birds and beasts of wild nature obtained by fowling and hunting"[28] and "game includes . . . animals pursued and taken by sportsmen . . . and are thus designated game for purposes of control and regulation of that pursuit."[29]

The courts of all the fifty states have long recognized that game animals are those which may be hunted. A species of animal normally classified as "game" may be temporarily, even permanently, removed from that designation under unusual circumstances. This would normally imply that a shortage in numbers has occurred and that these animals may be endangered. But, for the most part, game animals remain the objects of the hunt. This long and very clear tradition of treating animals as objects of the hunt suggests that hunting itself is clearly established in the law. Thus, we would conclude that it is wholly meaningless to suggest the existence of "game animals" without simultaneously implying the existence of hunters who will attempt to hunt these beasts.

The courts have had little interest in the hunt beyond the proper state regulations of reasons, firearms technology, bag limits and related items which are covered under game laws. The state has enforced property rights of hunters. An animal which is legally killed, or which would be legally killed if the hunt were not interrupted, belongs to that hunter.[30] Here the courts have merely recognized common law of long standing. Property rights over game animals are established by the successful hunt.[31]

The state's power to regulate hunting derives from two sources of authority. The first is its general police power, reserved to the states in the United States Constitution. The second source involves the power of the state to act, as sovereign, as trustee of certain collective properties for all of the people. Animals cannot themselves be owned so long as they exist *ferrae naturae,* but the right to hunt them resides collectively with the people in and through the state, subject only to reasonable state regulation.[32] The state could not generally prohibit hunting, unless there were some compelling reason, such as the public safety in a highly urbanized state. It might legitimately prohibit hunting of one or more species because of scarcity. The state has been held to have not only the power, but a specific duty, to regulate hunting of endangered species of animals.[32]

While a few commentators have held that "the right to kill game is a boon or privilege granted, either expressly or impliedly, by the sovereign authority, and is not a right inhering in any individual"[34] the law of the fifty states, as interpreted by their courts, seems to prove the contrary. A second authority, *Corpus Juris Secundum,* notes that "the right of hunting on public lands belongs in common to all members of the public."[35] The right to hunt on privately own- ed lands "is a property right in the owner of the soil, but is subject to the right of the state to regulate and preserve the game for public use."[36] The state may control, but not prohibit, hunting on private- ly owned lands by both owners and those to whom the owner has extended the privilege of hunting.

Whatever attempts the state might make to restrict or prohibit hunting, these laws and administrative regulations must be made within the limits on governmental power contained in state and the federal constitutions.[37] They must be defensible generally as a pro- per exercise of state police powers.[38] Game laws, by their very nature, and as noted above, must be designed to control huntable animals, and only within the context of hunting. That is to say that such game laws must be framed so as to protect the unreasonable and indiscriminate slaughter of the animals, permitting persons to hunt under reasonable restrictions that are designed to ensure the future of hunting.[39] Game laws apparently cannot be misused so as to prohibit hunting generally on grounds other than those designed to protect game animals.

Laws must be designed to ensure equal access to the hunt for all the citizens of a state. Each inhabitant must have an equal right to try to kill game. If foreigners are excluded from the hunt the pro- scription must be applied to all aliens, not just to a portion, or to certain races.[40] The same prohibition against discrimination applies to non-citizens of the state who are, however, American citizens. No sub-state government may use its power to exclude some state inhabitants and benefit the few. Regulation of hunting is preempted by states, save for nondiscriminatory regulation, mostly as proscrip- tions against hunting in municipalities or urban counties.

State courts have often been quite conscious of the growth of democratic rights generally, and, with reference to the present sub- ject, to the rights of citizens to hunt. In an 1896 decision[41] the Con- necticut Supreme Court noted the long struggle for citizen hunting rights. It quoted at length from experts such as the French legal philosopher Pothier. The court quoted Pothier's *Traité du droit de propertie* (headings 27-28) as follows: "Some ancient doctors have doubted if sovereigns had the right to reserve hunting to themselves and to forbid it to their subjects. They contend that as God has given man to man dominion over the beasts, the prince had no authority to deprive all his subjects of a right which God had given them." The court also quoted Blackstone's *Commentaries* which also noted the general rights of men to hunt in these words: "by the law of Nature, every man from the prince to the peasant has an equal right of pursuing and taking to his own use all such creatures as are *ferrae naturae* . . . but it follows from the very end and constitution of society that this natural right . . . may be restrained by positive laws . . . for the supposed benefit of the community."

What emerged from the *Geer* decision in Connecticut was a strong, pro-hunting opinion that differs little in substance or form from many other state high court decisions. The state may legitimately regulate certain aspects of hunting, and, as in this case, the interstate or intrastate transport of the meat. But the right to hunt is firmly entrenched in American law and culture. It cannot be systematically eroded or destroyed.

The *Geer* decision has its federal counterpart, but the federal case is less thorough and forceful.[42] Nevertheless, there seems to be a latent and residual federal right to hunt. This would be extended to lands under federal control, even if the federal rules contradicted state laws. The unfortunate dimension of the federal law is that there is no recognized right to hunt in all areas of federal land in which there is neither any scarcity of game, or where hunting would be no more dangerous than is common in other hunting areas.

For many years there seemed to be no area in which one could approach the United States Supreme Court to seek constitutional protection for the right to hunt. However, the expansive meaning given the Ninth Amendment in the last two decades[43] has offered a glimmer of hope for the protection of many unenumerated rights, including the right to hunt. There is no reason to assume that the high federal court will hear and decide favorably on such a broad allegation of right. Yet, one might suggest that the justices may continue to seek meaning in the Ninth Amendment beyond privacy and the right to have an abortion. I would think that quite an excellent case for the right to hunt, built on a long history of the right, might attract judicial notice. The primary problem here would be the establishment of judicial standing, a difficult thing to do in regard to forest rights.

For the present one must be content with a general assumption of the right as one claimed by the people as a natural right, but not yet fully protected legally or constitutionally. The existence of game laws, game wardens, game commissions, and game controls would seem to point toward the continued existence of the right to hunt.

Put another way, who would fund these things associated with game if not the hunter? The economic argument, in the long run, may be the strongest and best of all.

Our Endangered Wildlife

The great thrust of the anti-hunting movement has been directed at hunters who, it is alleged, are responsible for causing wildlife to disappear. There is no doubt that early man hunted those animals which were easiest to gather. If, in the process, whole species were destroyed, he could not have cared less. He simply moved on to other species and forgot about those which were destroyed. But modern man is somewhat different. He knows something of the world in which he lives, and he generally intends to protect it.

Animal species vanished long before man appeared on earth. Scientists know of many only by studying their remains. Collections of bones are gathered into museums the world over. It is an exciting day when a whole new species is discovered and catalogued and, if possible, mounted or reconstructed. But modern, thinking man has nothing to do with all of this in the sense of acting as agent. He can study these animals and give them names and hope to learn something about them. He can only offer hypotheses about why they died off.

The whole theory of evolution was developed to explain two cognate facts: the disappearance of some animals, and the appearance of some new ones. Presumably, whether by accretion over a period of time, or by sudden development, some animals leap forward into a new mold and appear as significantly different living beings. How and why this works is the proper subject for a whole field of knowledge.

Historic man, like the prehistoric precursors of man, killed off some species. He did so unconsciously, just as any other predator did, as a part of a grand a glorious chain of nature, perhaps fulfilling some role expected of him. With pre-man or man such animals as the giant sloth could co-exist only for a short while. It does very little good to catalogue such species destroyed by early man. My position on this is quite simiple. Man was a part of a predator-victim chain. The stronger survived. No plan for extermination existed. Early man was filling a role expected of him by nature. He was as caught up in this fate as were his victims. Man was not then capable of rationalizing his role. In this, he was much like any other predator that caused the unadapted to vanish.

It is not clear when man came to think of himself as wholly separate from the rest of Nature. It is unclear whether man, say, before the classical period of Greece and Rome, had ever intended to aestroy animals as a species. Certainly, there is an abundance of evidence that scarcity of game for the hunter is the normal condition of thinking, hunting man within recorded history. The Romans and the Greeks hunted animals beyond the conservationist's preference. The Romans probably did not destroy any whole species, but they did kill all or most of the members of certain species in certain areas. When the Romans withdrew some of the species reestablished themselves. The classic aristocratic answer to scarcity of game has always been to prohibit the lower classes from hunting.

There is some evidence, especially in the Book of Mormon, of early game preserves being established as a conservationist measure. Otherwise, game preserves were established generally to provide the king and the nobility with a sure hunting compound. Conservation is not a habit man learned early in his history.

The Survival Service Commission of the International Union for Conservation of Nature and Natural Resources has established the arbitrary date of 1600 A.D. as the base from which modern conservation can be measured. The Union's concern is for those species which have been made extinct, or which have become endangered since 1600. The *I.U.C.N. Bulletin,* a publication of the society, defends the date, pointing out several interesting things about their choice of times. By 1600 man had begun to identify the major species. Few, if any, of the species of vertebrates that have become extinct since 1600 are unidentified. We know something of those that have disappeared, such as their color, general size and the like. For the most of them a mounted specimen exists, and most were painted by some artist. Conversely, we know little about those other animals and birds that historic man has helped to kill off, or which have otherwise become extinct. Although some species have disappeared between the beginnings of recorded history and 1600, we know little about them.

The IUCNNR identifies some 4226 species of mammals living in 1600. There were then 8684 species of birds. Since that time 36 species of mammals and 94 of birds have disappeared and are considered to be extinct. An additional 120 animal species and 187 bird types are "red-lined" by the IUCNNR as in severe danger; it is possible that some have already vanished or are in such small numbers that extinction is foreordained by the circumstances. In short, about 1 percent of the total number of living bird and animal species, using 1600 as the base date, have disappeared forever, and another 3 percent are in grave danger.[1]

Man cannot be held responsible for many of these cases of extinction. Natural causes account for a portion. The theory of evolution teaches us that the average life expectancy for a species of mammals is just over a half a million years. A species of birds will, on the average, endure for two million years before dying off. New species emerge from some while others disappear without producing a durable offspring. In any period of time a certain number of animal and bird species can be expected to die off. This is an inexorable law of nature.

The reasons species disappear are many. Some become over-specialized and hence adapt only to very limited conditions. For example, a bird may live off only one type of bug. Its whole life is tied in with that one insect. If the insect dies off, so does the bird that lived off of it. Some species cannot adapt to even very slight changes in climate. Some cannot breed except under specified conditions. Change these conditions and the species dies off. Some types of animals, such as the mountain sheep, cannot compete with other types of animals such as the mountain goat. If the one assumes control over the territory of the other, the first one dies off.

Sometimes a whole ecology is built on very fragile grounds. There may have developed such a tight interlocking relationship that even one change threatens the entire chain of many species. The threat to this isolated ecology frequently comes from a change in specialization of one member of the community, or it comes from an artificially induced species from outside. This may occur due to a freak of nature, as when a new species is washed ashore in an unusual storm. More frequently man had a hand, albeit unwittingly, in it. Pigs or dogs may be washed ashore after a ship sinks, and these take up residence on the island where heretofore no pigs or dogs existed. Such was the fate of the famed Dodo bird.

Occasionally, nature will isolate or destroy. Floods, famines, diseases, and earthquakes are among the many natural occurrences that can wholly disrupt an ecology or destroy a species.

Man has upset ecologies by bringing in new species with which the native animals and birds cannot compete. The English sparrow and starling were introduced to the Americas and soon they spread, threatening many native species of birds. Man also introduced the hare to England and the rabbit to Australia, and other species to the East Indies, the West Indies, New Zealand other isolated areas. Some, like the rabbit, were deliberately introduced. Others, such as the rat, came without man's knowledge, but not as the result of such an accident as being washed ashore after a disaster. The southern portion of the United States has had problems with the nutria, introduced as a profitable fur bearer. Fire ants accidentally entered in shipments of vegetables. The list can grow indefinitely. Eventually, all such species can threaten the native species.

The destruction of habitat and changes in the general environment are major causes of species destruction. Man has improved his own environment by filling or draining swamps, but the whole fragile ecology is then threatened. Since some species exist only in a very confined area, a change in that one place may threaten all of that kind of animal life that exists in the world. The growing urban sprawl has caused shy creatures, such as the American bald eagle, to continue to withdraw until there is virtually nowhere left in the 48 contiguous states where it can or will live. The destruction of forests chase many animals away. The building of airfields, man-made lakes, parking lots, and cities have all changed the way animals may live. When one considers that less than 500 years ago a squirrel could travel from the American East Coast to the Mississippi without having to leave the treetops, one can see how the changes in environment have altered the way animals can live.

Man has changed the ecology in other ways. His chemicals make life for him more enjoyable, but sometimes at great cost to the animals of his environment. DDT was a major breakthrough, and its deadly effect on disease-carrying insects has helped to reduce many exotic and very disabling diseases such as malaria. However, these chemicals which are frequently not biodegradable can cause permanent damage to animal or bird life. DDT has been listed by the Department of the Interior as a major cause of destruction of American bald eagle eggs. The verdict is not in yet in many cases involving other chemicals. Indeed, we may one day find that some chemical considered safe today will have caused the extinction of some species of bird or mammal.

Occasionally, man sets about to destroy a species on purpose. If he could, man would probably destroy many predators and disease-carrying species, such as the common rat. In the off-beat history, *Rats, Lice and History,*[2] one author argues eloquently and well for a revised history of the West to show the great influences of animal-induced diseases. Without rats the great plagues, such as the Black Death, could not have been transmitted. Such avoidance of tragedy might have changed the whole course of history. It would be very difficult to find someone to defend the rat, although a scientist might still see its role as important in a general ecological system. Man has sought to eradicate whole species, however.

Farmers and ranchers frequently try to destroy predators which they blame for destruction of domesticated animals, and, occasionally, tag with the charge of man or child killer. In the American West the ranchers have made a concerted effort to de troy coyotes, mountain lions, wolves and other predators. Many state game commissions, pushed by some conservationists and farmers, have placed bounties on such animals as fox, wolves and pumas, and such birds as hawks and owls.

Many of the anti-predator efforts have been centered on the use of poisons. A secondary effect has been to kill off, as an undesired but nonetheless related event, other animals which eat or otherwise consume the poison. Rotting flesh left behind to attract coyotes may also attract hawks or bustards. Some animals upon which predators themselves feed are poisoned. Thus, a raccoon may eat the carcass of a poisoned groundhog, or a bustard may eat a poisoned prairie dog.

Some species exist in such a narrowly defined area that as little as a few square feet of space may contain all the members of that whole species. Such is the case with two small fish, one of which exists in only one well in the world, and even here, on one ledge in that one well. The snail darter exists in only one stretch of river and its protectors, including the federal government, have held up construction of a power dam so that the tiny fish might be preserved. Presumably, other similar species may have been accidentally or even purposefully destroyed in the advancement of mankind.

There is an intriguing question here. When making public policy decisions should the irrigation of a whole area be held up by the concern that an isolated species of fish may die off? Man must decide often between protecting some animal species and making progress in vital areas such as raising food, or providing power in a non-polluting manner. Let us pose another similar policy question. Should we continue to use DDT, presuming for a moment that no equally effective chemical exists, to eradicate insects that carry serious diseases, despite the fact that it may also destroy the last Ameri-

can bald eagle? Under the moral principle known as the two-fold effect, an undesired evil can be allowed if it is interconnected with a
good. By classic example, that principle permits the bombing of an
enemy ammunition dump (a good thing) even though the explosion
will probably kill patients in a nearby hospital (a bad thing).

Hunting accounts for the disappearance of some species of game
in historic times. Here, one must qualify the use of the term hunting
in order to arrive at a meaningful conclusion. We have previously
defined hunting to mean *sport* hunting, not indiscriminate slaughter
or market hunting. The English, European, and American practice
of killing large flocks of birds with a very large size shotgun ("punt
gun") is a relatively new development, having been made possible
only after the shotgun was fabricated. That happened only after our
base date of 1600. The shooter could discharge his weapon at a
flock settled on the ground or in the sky not to test his skill in drop-
ping a single bird, but to decimate the flock, to kill as many as possible.

The harvesting of many mammals by man has nothing to do with
hunting in the normal sense. Whales are harvested in huge numbers
because their oil and, to a degree, their flesh has a commercial market. Pre-technological man had no way to attack these mammals to
the extent that they would be endangered. Post-technological man
has the wherewithal to decimate the whale herds. To equate this
slaughter with the kind of hunting we have heretofore written of is
to miss the mark entirely. This slaughter falls within the same classification of market harvesting that caused the carrier pigeon to
become extinct. Such activity may be defensible, at least to the
degree that it does not destroy or endanger a whole species, but that
defense lies beyond the scope of this book.

The same point can be made about the annual harvests of the
baby seals in Canada and the other fur-bearing animals of the
world. The slaughter, to the degree that it only limits population,
may be a natural part of the life cycle of these species now. But this
harvest, despite the fact that it involves wild animals, does not fit
within our working definition of hunting.

Two other interrelated forms of collecting wild animals also lie
beyond the scope of our treatment. However, a brief discussion of
these forms of hunting does bear on the point that sport hunting has
not been among the principal causes of the extinction of animal
species since 1600. In 1965 there were 526 zoos in the world, all of
which competed for rare and exotic species of animals. This is dou-

ble the number of zoos that existed in 1945, and the number has since increased. This does not count the road-side and private zoos or collections of animals. Many species, such as the Chinese giant panda, will not reproduce in captivity, meaning that those specimens collected for zoos will die off without issue.

Private collectors seek to own exotic wildlife, many species of which are not truly suited to domesticated or semi-domesticated life. There is a flourishing trade in tropical birds and rare big cats and other unusual animals and birds. Beyond the fact that some present a health hazard — they carry diseases for which native species have little or no immunity — there is sometimes the great problem of endangering a species by collecting them for illegal sale to private parties.

Both zoos and individual collectors seek animals on the black market. In making such a general statement I do not mean to impugn the integrity of either reputable collectors or zoos. Still, the simple fact remains that individuials do collect and illegally sell rare birds and mammals. This suggests both an illegal source and an illegal market. The wholesale trade in exotic animals is large, involving millions of dollars every year according to IUCNNR. Some rare, tropical birds fetch several thousand dollars each in America and in Europe. Many unscrupulous zoos pay premium prices for specimens of rare birds and animals. Private, frequently unregulated zoos are also involved. A rare species is a guaranteed drawing card.

In tropical nations a significant portion of the national income may be derived from illegal sales of animals. It must be made very clear that not nearly all sales of exotic animals and birds are made in violation of government regulations to the contrary. Some petty dictatorships in Latin and Central America and Africa and Asia practice a national governmental policy of extermination of their wildlife resources. Desperate for hard foreign currency and lacking exploitable natural resources and agricultural surpluses, they turn to the illegal, immoral and highly profitable trade in rare animals. No international organization has the power to regulate such state practices.

Related to the problem of the collection of live animals for exhibition is the problem of the commercial killing of animals for some portion of their bodies. Again, this has been tied frequently to the public policy of states. Some African nations, notably the Centra African Republic and Uganda, have killed off herds of elephants for their ivory. Rare birds are slaughtered for their plumage. Crocodiles are killed for their skins. Big cats are hunted down for their hides. This list could be extended to include many other animals and birds. Sometimes it involves direct governmental policy; sometimes it is the result of individual acts of corrupt bureaucrats and the military; and sometimes it involves private persons given special license on payment of a fee, legal or illegal, to government. At the best, most underdeveloped and emerging nations lack the resources to carry out public policy generally. Against other public needs, such as building industry or feeding the population, protection of animals takes a very low priority. One writer likened the general situation to a weakened police force trying to establish order in a nation torn by riot, insurrection and sedition. The intention of the police may be good but they are powerless to overcome the obstacles to enforcement.[3]

Although we have established a base year of 1600 for our study of the destruction of animal species, we must note that, although Western man can be considered civilized by that arbitrary date, not all of the world's inhabitants are now or were then civilized. Of the ninety-four species of birds that have become extinct since 1600, only nine lived on continents. The remainder were inhabitants of islands, isolated in time and space, perhaps living an overspecialized existence and on borrowed time. Most of these species were destroyed by natural causes or accidentally induced condition, or by stone-age man. For example, from the first Polynesian colonization of New Zealand which occurred about 1000 A.D. until the first European settlements were established about 1800, some thirty-five or so species of birds were destroyed, largely by these aborigines. Since the arrival of Western civilization another nine types of birds have become extinct, but the role of the civilized men in this destruction has been minimal. Conversely, English and other colonizers have introduced an almost equal number of conditioned, but alien, species of birds and animals to New Zealand.

Many animals that are now endangered have been living on borrowed time for many centuries. The Pleistocene age officially ended about 10,000 years ago. Yet some highly specialized animals from that age still survive. Some of these animals have disappeared within the lifetime of thinking man. Examples would include the huge ground sloths and glyptodons of the Americas, and the over-sized elephants, lions, camels, bisons, and hippos of Europe and America. Others have been only very recently destroyed, such as the twelve-foot tall moas of New Zealand, the half-ton elephant birds of Madagascar, and similar super-birds of Micronesia and the East Indies. Still others, notably the large animals of Africa, such as hippos and elephants, are living anachronisms. While man's wasteful habits of overhunting may hasten the day when these are extinguished, the simple fact remains that they have lived beyond their own proper age.

After relieving thinking man of responsibility for the extermination of certain animals and birds, there does come a point at which we must face up to a certain responsibility the hunter must shoulder. No doubt, hunters have over-killed certain desirable species of animals. Trophy hunters have long sought certain elusive animals to kill as trophies, proofs of their prowess as hunters in seeking out a rare species and killing it. We are not referring to the commercial overkill of whales or the commercial exploitation of fur-bearers. We refer to the true hunting experience without commercial overtones.

While few members of the monkey family are hunted for sport, the great apes, notably the mountain gorilla, are occasionally hunted. Man at least occasionally kills some of these beasts for sport. Most of these killed are used by aborigines for food. The Mexican grizzly bear has been menaced by overhunting and by unregulated slaughter. A more telling factor may be the use of the poison sodium fluoroacetate (poison 1080), something unrelated to the hunt. Likewise, the polar bear has been threatened by both the sportsman and the native Aleutian hunter. Modern technology, which encourages hunting by airplane and powered boat, has removed much of the polar bear's natural defense of elusiveness. A Soviet authority, Dr. S.M. Uspensky, believes that rising Arctic water and general climatic conditions have had more of a negative influence on these animals than has hunting. The giant panda has been threatened to a small degree by hunting, but Communist China seems disposed to protect most of those remaining. It has been endangered more by its limited choice of territory than by hunting. A popular zoo attraction, the giant panda would be worth a great deal more alive when sold to such impoundments than it would be worth mounted in a hunter's den.

The giant otter has long been trapped and hunted for its pelt. It is listed on the IUCNNR's endangered species Red Sheet, but not because of sport hunting. The sea otter has been sought because of the value of its fur. The same is true of the Atlantic walrus, the ribbon seal, the Ross seal, the Mediterranean Monk Seal, the Caribbean Monk Seal, the Hawaiian Monk Seal, and other similar aquatic or semi-aquatic species. Some of these, along with the dugong, are hunted for oils and meat as well, but mostly by aborigines or by some commercial marketers.

The great cats are frequently hunted for sport, but the increasing value of their hides mark them for slaughter by commercial interests as well. Some are hunted even today as predators, despite their inclusion on IUCNNR and similar lists of endangered species. The Spanish lynx knows no closed or protected season. It enjoys protection only on a few government or private preserves. All dozen or so types of cougars are approaching extinction. Most were earmarked for extinction when they developed a taste for horses, cattle, and other domesticated animals. They came to prefer these easy victims to the more elusive prey upon which they had fed before. Still, some are hunted purely for sport, although commercial ranches have welcomed hunters. The Florida cougar exists only in isolated parts of the Everglades National Park, and even some of these are still killed when they venture out to kill on commercial farms. Cougars have a habit of retreating to trees when hunted with packs of dogs. once treed, they become, quite literally, sitting targets for hunters. The Asiatic lion differs little from its African cousin, and, indeed, many naturalists could not tell one from another. Whether a substantial difference exists or not, those lions that once lived in the Near East, Iran, perhaps Afghanistan, Pakistan, and India are nearly all gone. They are the victims of both hunting and advancing civilization. Natives fear them, tagging them with the title of child-killers. Governments, responding to popular pressures, have looked on benignly as hunters decimated their ranks. Some governments and political regimes have hired professionals to kill them off. Sport hunting can be held accountable to the degree that they are the willing accomplices of public officials and natives.

The tiger has shared much of the fate of the Asiatic, and, to some degree, the African lion. Its habitat has been reduced by man's encroachment. It too is generally considered to be a menace to human life. There are several varieties of tigers on the IUCNNR's Red List, including the Chinese, Bengali, Sumatran, Caspian, Siberian Javan, and Bali types. Sport hunting continues to take some toll, but the principal threats remain the reduction of habitat, commercial slaughter for hides, and the reduction of the menace to human beings.

Members of the wild ass, donkey, and horse families have been hunted to or near the point of extinction. Asiatic wild asses exist in at least five varieties. Some have been killed for meat, some captured and domesticated and most rounded up in some numbers to serve as superior breeding stock. African wild asses are eaten and domesticated, and only rarely hunted. Both Asian and African varieties have been reduced in numbers by two other extraneous factors: changes in habitat, especially where rainfall has lessened, and the intrusion of man with his managed herds of domesticated animals. Certain species of zebras have been hunted, largely by commercial interests for zoos, or by aborigines for meat; they are thus endangered.

Rhinos have long presented a challenge to the hunter, for, even with the most modern magnum rifles, a rhino is a dangerous and worthy object of the hunt. Among the threatened varieties of rhinos are the following: Great Indian, Sumatran, white (or square-lipped), and black. Again, the change of habitat, the intrusion of man and the spread of civilization, are among the chief causes of endangerment. Sport hunting has decimated the ranks of some types of rhinos, but more generally kills by aborigines and commercial hunters have had more effect. Some peoples believe that certain magic properties are to be found in the rhino horns and seek the powered horn for sexual or health purposes.

Certain species of the deer genus are also threatened. Some of these have been hunted extensively by sport hunters, but, again, the natives seek out certain species for table meat. Among those marked for extinction unless careful conservation is practiced are the following: Persian fallow deer, the Southeast Asian Brow-antlered deer, and the Formosan, North Chinese, Shansi and Ryuku sika deer. Some of these have been captured for zoos and some have been sold to commercial reserves to provide targets for paying customers who desire to kill exotic and unusual varities of deer.

Related to the varieties of deer we find the same to be true of the various kinds of antelopes and similar species. Long sought after by hunters are such endangered species as the giant Sable antelope, the Arabian oryx, the scimiatr-horned oryx, the addax, the bontebok, Hunter's hartebeest, and several varieties of gazelles. The exotic formation of horns makes the heads especially appealing to those hunters who like to line their dens with such proofs of the kill. But, for the most part, the usual conditions that go far beyond hunting have applied to these types of animal life. The hunter has played only a minor role in the endangerment of these species.

We could continue to list animal species which are endangered; and we have said little of those which are extinct already. The point remains the same. Man as a sport hunter, the archetype "white hunter," has played only one, frequently minor role in this great drama. One must look to aboriginal and commercial hunters and to a variety of natural conditions to find the bulk of the explanation for this series of disappearances of animal life.

The modern, educated hunter has a major stake in the survival of all huntable animals. Should the desirable and rare species die or be killed off, there would be no more for him or for future generations to hunt. It is suicidal to destroy species. The hunter recognizes that there is little challenge, thus little interest, when game is so plentiful that he can kill without effort. The difficulty of the hunt determines the value of the kill. The hunter recognizes that there will be no huge surplus of the most desirable animals in the future. He knows that he must act as a conservationist if any hunting is to be possible in the future.

The hunter is not interested in preservation of docile species in a zoo. Animals there lose their instincts and senses to such a degree that they are no longer the worthy objects of a hunt. Hunting is not constituted by merely looking at an animal behind a fence. The hunter needs to have animals survive in their native habitat; only there will they prove to be objects worthy of his attention.

To these ends, the hunter has sponsored and backed legislation designed to guarantee the continued existence of many forms of wildlife. He supports governmental and private action designed to propagate any and all huntable wildlife.

The good work of national and international wildlife organizations is undermined very rapidly by counter-productive measures taken by governmental or quasi-governmental organizations that seek only to exploit wildlife without considering the future. One thinks of the great evil caused by the remnants of Uganda dictator Idi Amin's army which destroyed elephant herds with rockets, machine guns and canon. This unraveled the work of generations of conservationists in one stroke. One can think of the planned extermination of other elephant and rhino herds by army units in other areas of Africa. Here, again, the cause of conservationists and hunters alike was undone.

The occasional wealthy sport hunter who buys and bribes his way into an area inhabited by an endangered species does the general cause of hunters great harm. Just as in any other area of human activity, there are those unscrupulous individuals who will violate the law to the detriment of both man and nature. But, fortunately, these incidents are rare.

For the most part the only animals threatened are those that live in isolated or severely confined areas of the world, or those which man fears. The supplies of the species of game man ordinarily hunts for sport have stabilized, as habitat permits. This is true of rabbits, squirrels, deer, and many varieties of birds. Elk, moose, bison and similar game are well managed and limited hunting is permitted.

Notes

ON THE PLEASURES OF HUNTING

This section is a condensation of and a commentary on Ortega y Gasset's *Meditations on Hunting*. I believe that it is noteworthy that, while there are many treatises on Ortega's general philosophy, the philosophical community has for the most part ignored this vital portion of Ortega's thought. That is indeed unfortunate for nowhere else is his idea of "I equals me plus my environment" so clearly stated in specific and concrete terms.

1. I ask the reader to consider Ortega's very clear and specific view of what the hunt is, against the very unspecific, general and confused views (which are certainly not definitions) offered by such anti-hunting works as Cleveland Amory's *Man Kind?* and Lewis Regenstein's *The Politics of Extinction*. Where Ortega properly distinguishes each vital element of the hunt from mere slaughter, the anti-hunters lump all killing of animals by humans into a generic term, "hunting." Amory's absurd idea of "arming bears" to retaliate against hunters demonstrates that confusion of ideas.

MAN THE HUNTER

1. See Glynn Isaac, "The Diet of Early Man" *World Archaeology* (February 1971); A.C. Leopold and Robert Ardrey, "Toxic Substances in Plants and the Food Habits of Early Man," *Science* (May 5, 1972).

2. See Robert Ardrey, *The Hunting Hypothesis* (New York, 1976), p. 58ff.

3. Among other works, see L.S.B. Leakey, "Bone-Smashing by Late Miocene Hominid," *Nature* (May 28, 1971), and Richard Leakey, "Further Evidence of Lower Pleistocene Hominids from Lake Rudolf," *Nature* (May 28, 1971); also, L.S.B. Leakey and Robert Ardrey, "Man the Killer," *Psychology Today* (September 1972). An excellent summary of the Leakdy family work can be found in Sonia Cole, *Leakey's Luck* (New York, 1975). L.S.B. Leakey's work is reported in volumes I and III of *Olduvai Gorge* (Cambridge, 1965, 71).

4. Michael and Sheilagh Crawford, *What We Eat Today* (London, 1972); and see also, M.A. Crawford and A.J. Sinclair, "Nutritional Influences in the Evolution of the Mammalian Brain," CIBA Foundation Symposium, October 1971.

5. Ardrey's work is extensive, sometimes controversial and, in many ways, revolutionary. I have accepted most of his basic theses, as are appropriate to this chapter and study, not only from *The Hunting Hypothesis* (New York, 1976), but from several other of his works: *The Social Contract* (1970), *The Territorial Imperative* (1966) and *African Genesis* (1961).

6. See Leakey and Ardrey, "Man the Killer," and Ardrey's *Hunting Hypothesis*, pp. 169-75.

HUNTING IN THE JUDAEO-CHRISTIAN TRADITION

1. *Tsud* is found in Gen. 27:5; Lev., 17:13; Job 10:16,38,39; Psalms 140:11; Prov. 6,26; Jer. 16:26 and 16:16; Mic. 7:2; Ezek. 13:18-20.

2. *tsadah* is found in 1 Sam. 24:11.

3. *radaph* is found in 1 Sam. 26:20.

4. *Tasyid* is found in Gen. 10:9, 25 and 27.

5. *Metsudah* is found in Ezek. 13:21.

6. Generally, see W.H. Bennett "Hunting" in James Hastings (ed) *A Dictionary of the Bible* (New York: Scribner's, 1903).

7. *Kethibh* is found in Gen. 21:20 and Gen. 25:27.

8. Generally, our approach follows that of Manfred O. Meitzen, "The Ethics of Hunting: A Christian Perspective," 16 *Dialog* (Winter 1977).

OUR HUNTING HERITAGE: EUROPE

1. Michael Brander, *Hunting and Shooting* (New York, 1971), pp. 12-24.

2. The major Roman writers, including Virgil, Cicero and Horace extolled the virtues of hunting and reported laws concerned with the hunt. The Greek general Xenophon wrote detailed instructions on horses and hounds used for hunting and talked of their care. He also offered advice on the selection of types of hounds for various kinds of hunting.

3. A convenient source for these old English laws is Dorothy Whitelock (ed), *English Historical Documents, c. 500-1042* (New York, 1951).

4. These later medieval documents are easily located in the second volume of the above, David C. Douglas (ed) *English Historical Documents, 1042-1189* (New York, 1953).

5. The text of the Assize of the Forest is found in *Ibid.,* pp. 418-20.

6. Assize of the Forest, Article I.

7. Assize of the Forest, Article III.

8. Assize of the Forest, Article IX.

9. Assize of the Forest, Article XI.

10. Assize of the Forest, Article VII.

11. "Dialogues de Scaccario" in Douglas, *op. cit.,* II, 490-569 at 528. This work was probably written by Richard FitzNigel, Chancellor of the Exchequer (1160-98), and was possibly composed c.1178.

12. W.A. Morris, *The Medieval English Sheriff to 1300* (Manchester, 1927).

General Notes

Some excellent general works on European hunting include the following which I consulted while searching this chapter: Michael Brander, *Hunting and Shooting* (New York, 1971); E.W.D. Cuming, *British Sport, Past and present* (London, 1909); John N. George, *English Guns and Rifles* (Plantersville, SC, 1947) and *English Pistols and Revolvers* (Plantersville, 1938); George Hanger, *To All Sportsmen, Farmers and Gamekeepers* (London, 1814); Guy E. Laking, *A Record of European Arms and Armour Through Seven Centuries* (5 vols; London, 1920-22); W. Keith Neal, *Spanish Guns and Pistols* (London, 1955); R. Ewart Oakeshott, *The Archaeology of Weapons* (London, 1960); Pierre-Louis Ducharte, *Histoire des armes de chasse et de leur emplois* (Paris, 1955); and J.F.C. Fuller, *Armament and History* (New York, 1945).

THE AMERINDIAN AND HUNTING

1. The obvious reference is to Robert F. Berkhofer Jr. *The White Man's Indian* (New York, 1978) wherein the author attempts to discover the difference between the real Amerindian and the picture of him artificially created by whites.

2. In general the treatment here follows orthodox views such as those expressed in Lewis O. Saum, *The Fur Trader and the Indian* (Seattle 1965); Arthur J. Ray, *Indians in the Fur Trade: Their Role as Trappers, Hunters and Middlemen in the Lands Southwest of the Hudson Bay 1660-1870.* (Toronto, 1974); Harold Hickerson, "Fur Trade, Colonialism and the North American Indians" in 1 *Journal of Ethnic Studies* (Summer 1973), pp. 15-44; and John McManus, "An Economic Analysis of Indian Behavior in the North American Fur Trade" 32 *Journal of Economic History* (March 1972), pp. 36-53.

3. See Frank Klingberg, "The Noble Savage as seen by the Missionaries of the Society for the Propagation of the Gospel in Colonial New York 1702-1750," 8 *Historical Magazine of the Protestant Episcopal Church* (June 1939), pp. 128-65. See various contemporary accounts by trappers, travellers and missionaries among the Amerindians, such as *Mundus Novus Albericus Vespucius Laurentin-to Petri de Medicis Salutem Plurimam Dicit.*

4. See W.H. Hutchinson, "Dissenting Voice Raised Against the Resurrection of the Myth of the Noble Savage."

5. See Maurice Wasserman, "The American Indian as seen by Seventeenth Century Chroniclers," University of Pennsylvania Ph.D. dissertation, 1954.

6. Wilcomb Washburn, "The Clash of Morality in the American Forest" in Fredi Chiapelli et al. (eds.) *First Images of America: The Impact of the New World on the Old* (Berkeley, 1976) I, pp. 335-350.

7. See Cornelius Jaenen, "The Frenchification and Evangelization of the Amerindians in Seventeenth Century New France" in 35 *Study Sessions* (1969), pp. 57-72.

8. See Martin Calvin, *Keepers of the Game: Indian-Animal Relations and the Fur Trade* (Berkeley, 1978); also his "The War Between the Indians and the Animals" in 87 *Natural History* (June/July 1978), pp. 92-96.

9. John H. Kennedy, *Jesuit and Savage in New France* (New Haven, 1950).

10. Francis Parkman, *The Jesuits in North America in the Seventeenth Century* (Boston, 1867); Francis Jennings, "Goals and Functions of Puritan Missions to the Indians," 18 *Ethnohistory* (September 1971), pp. 197-212; and R.P. Beaver "American Missionary Motivation Before the Revolution," 31 *Church History* (June 1962), pp. 216-26.

HUNTING AND THE AMERICAN EXPERIENCE

One of the best references on the subject is Charles F. Waterman, *Hunting in America* (New York, 1973), a book flawed by few errors of fact or date. As a bonus it is lavishly illustrated and beautifully done. Michael Brander's *Hunting and Shooting* (New York, 1971) has two excellent chapters on American hunting (chs. VI and IX), and is also well illustrated. *Outdoor Life's* regular staff has put together quite a good collection on various aspects of the subject under the title of *The Story of American Hunting and Firearms* (New York, 1959). The standard reference on early American firearms is Carl Russell, *Guns on the Early Frontier* (New York, 1957). An older, but excellent, reference on hunting generally is Raymond Camp's compilation of entries published as *The Hunter's Encyclopedia* (Harrisburg, Pa., 1948). A more recent book which sportsmen view with very

mixed sentiments because of its blatant bias against firearms ownership in contemporary America is Lee Kennett and Richard Anderson, *The Gun in America*
(New York, 1978). Nonetheless, it is quite valuable as a study of certain aspects of
hunting. Harold L. Peterson has probably contributed more toward an understanding of early American firearms and their role in American history than any
other single individual. One can easily recommend his books generally for clarity
of thought, expression, and description, as well as for absolute accuracy. One
book stands out, his *Treasury of the Gun* (New York, 1962). Two excellent
studies of Western rifles were done by Charles E. Hanson, Jr., *The Northwest
Gun* (Lincoln, NB, 1955) and *The Plains Rifle* (Harrisburg, PA., 1960).

There are number of excellent studies of individual weapons, such as the Colt,
Sharps, Remington, Smith & Wesson, and so on, all of which, to a greater or
lesser degree, contributes to our knowledge of improvements in hunting brought
on by breakthroughs in technology. A representative sampling would include:
Claude Fuller, *The Breech-loader in Service* (Topeka, KS., 1933) and *The Rifled
Musket* (Harrisburg, PA, 1958); Arcadi Gluckman, *U.S. Martial Pistols and
Revolvers* (Buffalo, 1939) and *U.S. Muskets, Rifles and Carbines* (Buffalo,
1948); James J. Grant, *Single Shot Rifles* (New York, 1947), and *More Single
Shot Rifles* (New York, 1959); Alden Hatch, *Remington Arms* (New York, 1956);
Henry J. Kauffman, *The Pennsylvania-Kentucky Rifle* (Harrisburg, 1960); Joe
Kindig, Jr., *Thoughts on the Kentucky Rifle in Its Golden Age* (Wilmington, DL,
1960); Waldo E. Nutter, *Manhattan Arms* (Harrisburg, 1958); Ned Roberts, *The
Muzzle-loading Cap-lock Rifle* (Harrisburg, 1952); James E. Serven, *Colt
Firearms* (Santa Ana, CA, 1954); Winston O. Smith, *The Sharps Rifle* (New
York, 1943); Harold E. Williamson, *The Winchester: The Gun That Won The
West* (Washington, 1952); and Lewis Winant, *early Percussion Firearms* (New
York, 1959).

There are many good books dealing with the hunting of individual species of
game. A representative sample would include: Wayne Gard, *The Great Buffalo
Hunt* (New York, 1960); Francis Haines, *The Buffalo* (New York, 1970); Frank
C. Hibben, *Hunting American Bears* (Philadelphia, 1945); U.S. Department of
the Interior, *Wildfowl Tomorrow* (1964); Francis H. Kortright, *The Ducks,
Geese and Swans of North America* (Harrisburg, 1942); and Walter O. Taylor,
ed., *The Deer of North America* (Harrisburg, 1956). Several more general books
deserve notice: Durward L. Allen's *Our Wildlife Legacy* (New York, 1956) is a
magnificent book which is full of vital information for generalist and specialist
alike. Others include: Carleton S. Coon, *The Hunting Peoples* (Boston, 1971);
George Laycock, *The Alien Animals* (Garden City, NY, 1966); National Geographic Society, *Wild Animals of North America* (Chicago, 1960); James B.
Trefechen, *Crusade for Wildlife* (Harrisburg, 1961) and Herbert Manchester,
Four Centuries of Sport in America (New York, 1931).

HUNTING AND ETHICS

1. Among the better known works would be several of Robert Ardrey's, including *African Genesis* (1961); *The Territorial Imperative* (1966), and *The Social
Contract* (1970); see also, Adriaan Kortlandt, "Bipedal Armed Fighting in Chim-
panzees," XVI *Symposium* of Congress of Zoology, vol. 3, 1963; "Protohomi-
nid Behavior in Primates," X *Symposium* of the Zoological Society (August
1963); W.H. Thorpe, "Comparison of Vocal Communications in Animals and
Men" in R.A. Hunde (ed) *Non-Verbal Communication* (Cambridge University
Press, 1962); J.D. Fleming, "The State of the Apes," *Psychology Today*

(January 1974); C.R. Carpenter, *Naturalistic Behavior of Nonhuman Primates* (Penn State University, 1964); Konrad Lorenz, *On Aggression* (New York, 1966); and, Edward O. Wilson, *Sociobiology: The New Synthesis* (New York, 1975).

2. Among these are Cleveland Amory, *Man Kind? Our Incredible War on Wildlife* (New York, 1974); Patricia Curtis, *Animal Rights* (New York, 1980); James Dewar, *The Rape of Noah's Ark* (London, 1969); Joel Feinberg, "The Rights of Animals and Unborn Generations" in William Blackstone (ed) *Philosophy and Environmental Crisis* (University of Georgia Press, 1974); Michael W. Fox, *Towards the New Eden: Animal Liberation* (New York, 1979); Mel Morse, *On the Fifth Day: Animal Rights and Human Ethics* (Washington, 1978); Tom Regan (ed), *Matters of Life and Death* (New York, 1979); and Tom Regan and Peter Singer (eds), *Animal Rights and Human Obligations* (Englewood Cliffs, 1976).

3. David R. Klein, "The Ethics of Hunting and the Antihunting Movement" 38 *Transactions* of North American Wildlife and Natural Resources Conference (March 1973), pp. 256-67.

4. Some of the antihunting literature surveyed includes the following: Amory, *op. cit.;* Harold E. Anthony and Joseph Wood Krutch, "The Sportsman or the Predator?" *Saturday Review* (August 17, 1957), pp. 9-12, 40-41; Don Atyeo, "The Killer Urge," *Chic,* (October 1979), pp. 61-93; Nelson Bryant, "Behold the Hunter," *Atlantic Monthly* (December 1977), pp. 66-70; A.A. Ellison, "The Sport of Killing," *Boston Globe* (Feb. 25, 1972); Jim Harrison, "Grim Reapers of the Land's Bounty," 35 *Sports Illustrated* (1971), pp. 38-40, 43-44, 48; Charlene Heinen, "Answering the Hunters," 4 *Mainstream* (1966), pp. 5-6; Vincent A. Holmes-Gore, *These We Have Not Loved* (Essex, 1971); John Hoyt, "Special Report on Hunting" (Humane Society of U.S., Sept. 1972); Monica M. Hutchings and Mavis Caver, *Man's Dominion: Our Violation of the Animal World* (London, 1970); Brad Kennedy, 'It's Not the Hunters," *New York Times* (June 26, 1979)' Ernest W. Martin, *The Case Against Hunting* (London, 1959); John G. Mitchell, "Bitter Harvest: Hunting in America," *Audubon Magazine* (May 1979 through January 1980); Patrick Moore (ed), *Against Hunting* (London, 1965); Gene Mueller, "Blood Sport: The Firing Grows Louder," *Washington Star* July 20, 1978); Henry Romney, "How to Reform Hunters," 13 *Sports Illustrated* (Nov. 1960), pp. 66-69; Pat Ryan, ". . . And a Partridge in a Pear Tree," 34 *Sports Illustrated* (Feb. 1971); George B. Shaw, "Killing for Sport" in L. Hamalian and E.L. Volpe (eds), *Great Essays by Nobel Prize Winners* (New York, 1960); and Roger Williams "The Politics of Wild Animals," *World* (Feb. 13, 1973), pp. 24-27.

5. Pierre Teilhard de Chardin, *Works* (9 vols. projected; Paris, 1955---) *The Phenomenon of Man* (trans. by Bernard Wall; New York, 1959); see also, R.T. Francoeur (ed) *The World of Teilhard* (Baltimore, 1961) and C. Tresmontant, *Pierre Teilhard de Chardin: His Thought* (Baltimore, 1959).

6. Albert Schweitzer, *The Animal World of Albert Schweitzer* (ed., trans. by C.R. Joy; Boston, 1951), and Schweitzer's *The Philosophy of Civilization* (trans. by C.T. Campion; New York, 1964).

ANIMAL RIGHTS?

1. See George Boas, *The Happy Beast in French Thought of the 17th Century* (New York, 1966); see also, Gerald Carson, *Men, Beasts and Gods: A History of Cruelty and Kindness to Animals* (New York, 1972); Dix Harwood, *Love for Animals and How It Developed in Great Britain* (Columbia U. Ph.D. disserta-

tion, 1928); Hester Hastings, *Man and Beast in French Thought of the 18th Century* (Johns Hopkins Studies in Romance Literatures and Language, 1936); Mary Midgley, *Beast and Man: The Roots of Human Nature* (Ithaca, NY, 1978); and Terence H. White, *The Book of Beasts* (ed., trans., from 12th century MS; London, 1956).

2. Bernard de Mandeville, *The Fable of the Bees* (London, 1723).

3. See Richard D. French, *Antivivisection and Medical Science in Victorian Society* (Princeton, 1975) and Ernest S. Turner, *All Heaven in a Rage* (London, 1964).

4. Several other mainstream Christian interpretations include: Dom Ambrose Agius, *God's Animals* (London, 1970); Stephen R.L. Clark, *The Moral Status of Animals* (Oxford, 1977); Vincent A. Holmes-Gore, *These We Have Not Loved* (Essex, 1971); Edward Johnson, *Species and Morality* (Princeton U. Ph.D. dissertation, 1976); Charles W. Hume, *The Status of Animals in the Christian Religion* (London, 1957).

5. Salt's *Animals' Rights* have recently been reissued by the Society for Animal Rights (1980) with an annotated bibliography. The University of Illinois published George Hendrick's biography, *Henry Salt: Humanitarian, Reformer, Man of Letters* in 1977.

6. From Salt's response to Ritchie, an appendix to the 1895 edition of Salt's book.

7. See Dagobert DeLevie, *The Modern idea of Prevention of Cruelty to Animals and Its Reflection in English Poetry* (New York, 1947).

8. See also Heini Hediger, *Man and Animal in the Zoo* (New York, 1969) and, by the same author, *Wild Animals in Captivity* (New York, 1950).

9. *Report of the Technical Committee to Enquire into the Welfare of Animals Kept Under Intensive Livestock Husbandry Systems* (London: Command Paper 2836, 1965).

10. Cleveland Amory, *Man Kind? Our Incredible War on Wildlife* (New York, 1974), see pp. 3ff.

THE RIGHT TO HUNT AND NATIONAL DEFENSE

The Arthur D. Little Report to the United States Army on the Activities and Missions of the National Board to Promote Rifle Practice exists only in the five original copies noted in the text, and in an unknown, but very limited number of photoduplicated copies. The summary of the report consisting of Chapter I and II, in addition to the National Rifle Association copies, appears as part II of my *Citizen Soldier and United States Policy* (North River Press, Croton-on-Hudson, NY, 1979). Few Congresspersons know of its existence. As a graduate student working on a dissertation on the right to keep and bear arms, I was interested in obtaining a copy. After great difficulty I was able to obtain the summary, not from government, but from the NRA. It was not until 1979 that I ever saw the whole report. Much of the information about the making of the report has come through private correspondence since the *Citizen Soldier* was published, and is here printed for the first time. While there is an almost unending volume of material on the failures of the militia-National Guard programming, there is a scarcity of published material on the preinduction training of young men through hunting and shooting programs. Yet, I consider this to be especially important as a main line of support for continuation of such programming and in the maintenance of the rights to shoot and to hunt. The Supreme Court in *United States v. Miller* (307 US 174) and elsewhere gave great support to the proposition that the right to shoot, and with it the right to hunt, existed primarily, if not exclusively, because of the necessity to create and maintain a pool of manpower trained and skilled in shooting skills. Yet this line of reasoning has not generally been carried to its logical conclusion — that shooting and hunting educational programs must be supported.

THE LEGAL RIGHT TO HUNT

1. An excellent summary of this is found in *Greer v. Connecticut*, 87 Conn 519 (1895).
2. *Missouri v. Holland*, 252 U.S. 416 (1920).
3. *In re Blackbird*, 109 F. 139.
4. *Organized Village of Kake v. Egan*, 80 S Ct 33 (1959).
5. Regulation of hunting "is an exercise of a state's sovereignty." *People v. Chosa*, 233 N.W. 205.
6. *In re Eberle*, 98 F. 295.
7. *Patsone v. Pa*, 34 S Ct 281.
8. *State v. Tower*, 24 A. 898.
9. *Shively v. Bowlby*, 152 U.S. 1; *State v. McCullagh*, 96 Kan 786; *State v. Sawyer*, 113 Me 4589; *Musgrove v. State*, 236 Miss 513.
10. *Ex parte Kenneke*, 136 Cal 527; *Smith v. State*, 155 Ind 611; *State v. Weber*, 102 SW 955; *Fields v. Wilson*, 207 P 2d 153; *State v. Pollock*, 175 NW 557; *Graves v. Dunlap*, 152 P 532.
11. *Ex parte Peterson*, 119 Cal 578, 51 P 859.
12. *Hamilton v. Williams*, 200 So 80; *State v. Clement* 178 So 493; *Winslow v. Fleischner*, 233 P 922.
13. *Kellogg v. King*, 46 P. 166; *Glenn v. Kays*, 1 Ill. App. 479; *Rosenthal-Brown Fur Co. v. Jones-Frere Fur Co.*, 110 So 630; *Buras v. Salinovich*, 97 So 748.
14. Generally, the right to hunt on private land is subject to whatever conditions the landowner wishes to stipulate, *Council v. Sanderlin*, 111 S.E. 365; *Anderson v. Gipson*, 114 S.W. 2d 948.
15. *State v. Evans*, 152 N.E. 776.
16. *Graves v. Dunlap*, 152 P. 532.
17. *State v. Evans*, 152 N.E. 776.
18. See *Blades v. Hicks*, 11 H.L. Cases 621 (18645); *State v. Mallory*, 83 S.W. 955; *Hanson v. Fergus Falls National Bank & Trust*, 65 N.W. 2d 857.
19. The term actually appears late in Rome, in *The Digest*, Book 41, title 1, *De Adquir. Rer. Dom.;* see also Justinian's *Institutes* (ed. comp. by Tribonian), Book 2, Title 1, s. 12.
20. *State v. Taylor*, 72 Am. Dec. 347, 27 N.J.L. [3 Dutch] 117.
21. *State v. Hume*, 95 P. 808.
22. *Gray v. Stoutamire*, 178 So 730.
23. *Andrews v. Smith*, 188 Atl. 146.
24. *People v. Dello*, 71 N.Y.S. 2d 145.
25. *Fields v. Wilson*, 207 P. 2d 153.
26. *Graves v. Dunlap*, 152 P. 532.
27. *McMahon v. State*, 97 N.W. 1035.
28. *People v. O'Neil*, 39 N.W. 1; see also, *Meul v. People*, 64 N.E. 1106.
29. *State v. Iliggins*, 28 S.E. 15.
30. *Dapson v. Daly*, 153 N.E. 454; *Pierson v. Post*, 2 Am. Dec. 264; *Liesner v. Wanie*, 145 N.W. 374.

31. *Dapson v. Daly, supra.*
32. *Begay v. Sawtelle,* 88 P 2d 999.
33. *Corron v. State,* 10 N.Y.S. 2d 960.
34. 35 *Amer. Jur. 2d* 671.
35. 38 *Corpus Juris Secondum* 4.
36. 38 *Corpus Juris Secundum* 3.
37. *State v. Bryan,* 99 So 327; *Commonwealth v. Graber.* 2 Monroe L.R. 91.
38. *Shouse v. Moore,* 11 F. Supp. 784; *State v. Rathbone,* 100 P. 2d 86.
39. *State ex rel. Oglesby v. Hand,* 119 So 376.
40. *Re Ah Chong* 2 F. 733.
41. *Geer v. Conn., supra.*
42. *Spring Valley Water Works v. Schottler,* 110 U.S. 347.
43. *Griswold v. Conn.* 381 U.S. 479; *Roe v. Wade,* 410 U.S. 113.

OUR ENDANGERED WILDLIFE

1. The ten most endangered species in the United States are: (1) Kuauai oo (bird). Habitat: Hawaii. Number surviving: about 4. (2) Dusky Seaside Sparrow (bird). Habitat: Coastal Florida. Number surviving: 13. (3) Clay-loving phacelia (flower). Habitat: Utah. Number surviving: 4. (4) Houston toad. Habitat: Southeast Texas. Number surviving: 1500. (5) Red Wolf. Habitat: Southern states. Number surviving: unknown. (6) Birdwing pearly mussel. Habitat; Tennessee River. Number surviving: unknown. (7) Kemps Ridley sea turtle. Habitat: Southern California and Mexico (beaches). Number surviving: several hundred. (8) Lotus blue butterfly. Habitat: California bogs. Number surviving: unknown. (9) Snail Darter. Habitat: Tennessee River. Number surviving: unknown. (10) Black-footed ferret. Habitat: Great Plains. Number surviving: unknown.

2. Hans Zinsser, *Rats, Lice and History* (Boston, 1935).

3. In James Fisher et al., *Wildlife in Danger* New York, 1969), p. 17.

General References

There is no scarcity of books on the various endangered species of wildlife. Most are listed and illustrated and described in standard books of animals and birds of the world or of specific areas of the world. The Fisher book (See footnote 2) is one excellent source. So is the *I.U.C.N. Bulletin.* Older sources of importance include: Glover M. Allen, *Extinct and Vanishing Mammals of the Western Hemisphere with the Marine Species of all Oceans* (New York, 1942); Francis Harper,*Extinct and Vanishing Mammals of the Old World* (London, 1945); and James C. Greenway, jr., *Extinct and Vanishing Birds of the World* (New York, 1958). On primitive man and aboriginal man as hunter, see, Robert Ardrey, *The Hunting Hypothesis* (New York, 1978); Hans Bandi, *Eskimo Prehistory* (Seattle, 1969); Saxton Pope, *A Study of Bows and Arrows* (Berkeley, 1923); Grahame Clark, *The Stone Age Hunters* (New York, 1967); and, Carleton Coon, *The Hunting Peoples* (Boston, 1971). Other useful works include: James B. Trefethen, *Crusade for Wildlife* (Harrisburg, PA, 1961); National Geographic Society, *Wild Animals of North America* (Chicago, 1960); Francis H. Kortright, *The Ducks, Geese and Swans of North America* (Harrisburg, 1942); Nicholas Point, *Wilderness Kingdom* (New York, 1967); Clifford Simak, *Tribolite, Dinosaur and Man* (New York, 1966); Michael Brander, *Hunting and Shooting* (New York, 1971); C.F.G.R. Schwerdt, *Hunting, Hawking, Shooting* (London, 1928, 4 vols.); and J. Drummond, *The Animals of New Zealand* (London, 1905).

Bibliography

Abridgements of the Patent Specifications Relating to Firearms and Other Weapons, Ammunition and Accouterments from 1558-1858. London, 1960.

Agius, Don Ambrose. *God's Animals.* London, 1970.

Allen, Durward L., *Our Wildlife Legacy.* New York, 1962.

Allen, Glover M. *Extinct and Vanishing Mammals of the Western Hemisphere with the Marine Species of All the Oceans.* New York, 1942.

American Game Conference of the Wildlife Management Institute. *American Game Policy and Its Development.* Washington, 1930.

Amory, Cleveland. *Man Kind? Our Incredible War on Wildlife.* New York, 1974.

Applegate, James E. "Attitudes Toward Deer Hunting in New Jersey: A Second Look." 3 *Wildlife Society Bulletin* 1 (Spring 1975): 3-6.

————. "Some Factors Associated with Attitude Toward Deer Hunting in New Jersey Residents." *Transactions* of the 38th North American Wildlife and Natural Resources Conference (1973): 267-273.

Auxter, Thomas. "The Right Not to be Eaten." 22 *Inquiry* (Spring-Summer 1979).

Bailey, James A., Elder, William, and McKinley, Ted (eds). *Readings in Wildlife Conservation.* Washington, 1974.

Barr, James. "Man and Nature: The Ecological Controversy and the Old Testament." *Ecology and Religion in History.* New York, 1974.

Batten, Peter. *Living Trophies: A Shocking Look at the Conditions in America's Zoos.* New York, 1976.

Becker, Earnest. "Toward the Merger of Animal and Human Studies." 4 *Philosophy of the Social Studies* (June-Sept. 1974): 235-254.

Blummer, Joseph T. *Life Style Characteristics of the Hunter.* Albuquerque, 1971.

Boas, George. *The Happy Beast in French Thought of the Seventeenth Century.* New York, 1966.

Boone and Crocket Club. *North American Big Game.* Pittsburgh, 1971.

Boone, R.P. "Deer Management on the Kaibab." *Transactions* of the Third Wildlife Conference of North America (1938): 368-375.

Bradford, Nettie. "Property Rights of Animals." 37 *Bulletin of the University of Utah* 9 (1946).

Brambell Report. *Report of the Technical Committee to Enquire into the Welfare of Animals Kept under Intensive Livestock Husbandry Systems.* Her Majesty's Command Paper No. 2836. London, 1965.

Branch, E.D. *The Hunting of the Buffalo.* New York, 1929.

Brander, Michael. *Hunting and Shooting.* New York, 1971.

Broadie, Alexander and Pybus, Elizabeth. "Kant's Treatment of Animals." 49 *Philosophy* (Oct. 1974): 375-383.

Brown, E.K. "Mountain Sheep Restoration in the Western States." *Proceedings* of the 26th Annual Conference of Western State Game and Fish Commissions. (1946): 76-82.

Brown, Louis G. and Yeager, Lee E. "Survey of the Illinois Fur Resources." 22 *Illinois Natural History Survey Bulletin* 6: 435-504.

Burch, Robert W. "Animals, Rights and Claims." 8 *Southwestern Journal of Philosophy* (Summer 1977).

Butler, Samuel. *Erewhon and Erewhon Revisited* (Chs. 26-27). New York: Random House, Modern Library, 1955.

Calahane, Victor H. "Shall We Save the Large Carnivores?" 11 *Living Wilderness* 17 (1946): 17-21.

Camp, Raymond (ea.), *The Hunter's Encyclopedia.* Harrisburg, 1948.

Caras, Roger. *Death as a Way of Life.* Boston, 1968.

Carhart, Arthur H. "Fallacies in Winter Feeding of Deer." *Transactions* of the 8th North American Wildlife Confernce (1943): 333-337.

Carrighan, Sally. *Wild Heritage.* Boston, 1965.

Carter, Harlon, "The Eleventh Commandment." *Petersen's Hunting* (June 1977): 20-21.

Catlin, George. *Illustrations of the Manners, Customs and Conditions of the North American Indians.* 2 vols. London, 1845.

Chapline, W.R. and Cooperrider, C.K. "Climate and Grazing." U.S. Department of Agriculture *Yearbook.* Washington, D.C., 1941.

Clapper, Louis S. "Hunting and Conservation." *National Wildlife Federation,* 1975.

Clark, Stephen R.L. "Animal Wrongs." 38 *Analysis* 3 (June 1978): 147-149.

————. "The Rights of Wild Things." 22 *Inquiry* (Spring-Summer 1979).

Clarke, C.H.D. "Autumn Thoughts of A Hunter." 22 *Journal of Wildlife Management* 4 (1969): 420-427.

Clarke, Francis (ed.). *Poetry's Plea for Animals: An Anthology of Justice and Mercy for Our Kindred in Fur and Feather.* Boston, 1927.

Clepper, Henry. *The Origins of American Conservation.* New York, 1966.

Cohen, Noah J. The Concept of Tsa'ar Ba'ale Hayyim: Its Bases and Development in Biblical, Midrashic and Talmudic Literature. Catholic University Press, 1953.

Coon, Carleton. *The Hunting Peoples.* Boston, 1971.

Cowan, Ian McT. 'The Timber Wolf in the Rocky Mountain National Parks of Canada." 25 *Canadian Journal of Research* (1947): 139-174.

DeLevie, Dagobert. *The Modern Idea of Prevention of Cruelty to Animals and Its Reflection in English Poetry*. New York, 1947.

Dewar, James. *The Rape of Noah's Ark*. London, 1969.

Dichter, Anita. "Legal Definitions of Cruelty and Animal Rights." 7 *Boston College Environmental Affairs Law Review* 1 (1978).

Dodge, Natt N. "Wildlife of the American West" in Jay Monaghan (ed.), *The Book of the American West*. New York, 1960.

Doig, Herbert E. "The Hunting Ethic." XXVI *Conservationist* 2 (1971): 15-16.

Ducharte, Pierre-Louis. *Histoire des arms de chasse et de leur emplois*. Paris, 1955.

Edminster, Frank C. "The Effect of Reforestation on Game." *Transactions* of the 21st North American Wildlife Conference (1935): 313-318.

Eliot, Robert. "Regan on the Sorts of Beings That Can Have Rights." 16 *Southern Journal of Philosophy* (Spring 1978): 701-705.

Elton, Charles and Nicholson, Mary. "The Ten Year Cycle in Numbers of the Lynx in Canada." 11 *Journal of Animal Ecology* 2 (1942): 215-244.

Errington, Paul L. *Of Predation and Life*. Iowa State University, 1967.

Evans, Edward. *The Criminal Prosecution and Capital Punishment of Animals*. London, 1906.

Evans, Thomas R. "What About Those Predators?" 11 *Conservation Volunteer* 64 (1948): 81-84.

Feinberg, Joel. "The Rights of Animals and Unborn Generations." *Philosophy and Environmental Crisis*. Athens, Georgia, 1974.

Field-Fisher, Thomas G. *Animals and the Law*. London, 1964.

Fisher, James; Simon, Noel; and Vincent, Jack. *Wildlife in Danger*. New York, 1969.

Fitch, Henry S. "A Study of Coyote Relationships on Cattle Range." 12 *Journal of Wildlife Management* (1948): 73-78.

Fowler, Corbin. "Freedom: Animal Rights, Human Rights and Superhuman Rights."4 *Auslegung* (1976).

_____. "Animal Liberation: A Critique." 88 *Ethics* (Jan. 1978).

_____. "Animal Suffering and Rights." 88 *Ethics* (Jan. 1978): 134-138.

Fox, Michael W. *Towards the New Eden: Animal Rights and Human Liberation.* New York, 1979.

Fox, Robin and Tiger, Lionel. *The Imperial Animal.* New York, 1971.

Frey, R.G. "Interests and Animal Rights." 27 *Philosophical Quarterly* (June 1977): 186-189.

Fuller, B.A.G. "The Messes Animals Make in Metaphysics." 46 *The Journal of Philosophy* (Dec. 1949): 829-838.

Gabrielson, Ira N. *Wildlife Conservation.* New York, 1943.

Garretson, Martin S. *The American Bison.* New York, 1938.

Garrett, James. *Characteristics of Nevada Hunters.* University of Nevada— Reno Agricultural Station Bulletin No. 22, 1970.

Geist, Valerius. "Neanderthal the Hunter." 90 *Natural History* 1 (Jan. 1981): 26-36.

Giles, Robert (ed.). *Wildlife Management Techniques.* Washington, D.C., 1969.

Godlovitch, Roslind. "Animals and Morals." 46 *Philosophy* (Jan. 1971): 23-33.

Gottschalk, John. "The German Hunting System." XXXVI *Journal of Wildlife Management* 1 (1968): 110-118.

Graham, Frank Jr. *Man's Domain.* Philadelphia, 1971.

Grange Wallace B. *The Way to Game Abundance.* New York, 1949.

Greenway, James C., Jr. *Extinct and Vanishing Birds of the World.* New York, 1958.

Grene, Marjorie. "People and Other Animals." 3 *Philosophical Forum* (Winter 1972): 157-172.

Griffin, Donald R. *The Question of Animal Awareness.* New York: Rockefeller University Press, 1976.

Harper, Francis. *Extinct and Vanishing Mammals of the Old World.* New York, 1945.

Hartshorne, Charles. "The Rights of the Sub-human World." *Environmental Ethics* (Jan. 1979): 49-60.

Hasker, William. "The Souls of Beasts and Men." 10 *Religious Studies* (Sept. 1974): 265-277.

Hediger, Heini. *Man and Animal in the Zoo.* Trans. by G. Vivers and W. Reade. New York, 1969.

————. *Wild Animals in Captivity.* Trans. by G. Sircom. New York, 1950.

Hendee, Hohn C. and Schoenfeld, Clay (eds.). *Human Dimensions in Wildlife Programs.* Washington, D.C., 1973.

Hickerson, Harold. "Fur Trade, Colonialism and the North American Indians." 1 *Journal of Ethnic Studies* (Summer 1973): 15-44.

Holmes-Gore, Vincent A. *These We Have Not Loved.* Essex, 1971.

Hornaday, William T. "The Extermination of the American Bison." *Annual Report* of the U.S. Museum of Natural History (1887): 367-548.

Hume, Charles W. *The Status of Animals in the Christian Religion.* London, 1957.

Hutchings, Monica M. and Caver, Mavis. *Man's Dominion: Our Violation of the Animal World.* London, 1970.

Kirkpatrick, Thomas O. *The Economic and Social Values of Hunting in New Mexico.* University of New Mexico Bureau of Business Research, Monograph, 1965.

Klein, David R. "The Ethics of Hunting and the Antihunting Movement." *Transactions* of the 38th North American Wildlife and Natural Resources Conference (1973): 257-267.

Klaits, Joseph, and others (eds.). *Animals and Men in Historical Perspective.* New York, 1974.

Klessig, L.L. "Hunting in Wisconsin." M.S. Thesis, University of Wisconsin, Madison, 1970.

Kortright, Francis H. *The Ducks, Geese and Swans of North America.* New York, 1949.

Krug, Alan Scott. "The Socio-economic Impact of Firearms in the Field of Conservation and Natural Resources Management." *Pennsylvania Cooperative Wildlife Research Paper No. 118* (1965).

Laycock, George. *The Alien Animals.* Garden City, N.Y., 1966.

Lowry, Jon. "Natural Rights: Men and Animals." 6 *Southwestern Journal of Philosophy* (Summer 1975): 109-122.

Lee, Richard and Devore, Irven (eds.). *Man the Hunter.* Chicago, 1966.

Leopold, Aldo. *Sand County Almanac.* New York, 1949.

_____. *Game Management.* New York, 1933.

_____. "Wildlife in American Culture." 7 *Journal of Wildlife Management* (1943) 1: 1-6.

Lumsden, H.G. "The Problem of Changing Beliefs and Attitudes." 21 *Journal of Wildlife Management* 4 (1957): 463-465.

Lund, Thomas A. *American Wildlife Law.* University of California, 1980

Lundy, Herbert. "The Hunters." 1 *Nevada Outdoors Wildlife Review* 4 (1957): .3-15, 22, 24, 26.

Madison, John. "The Hunters." 13 *Maine Fish and Game* 4: 20-23.

Margolis, Joseph. "Animals Have No Rights and Are Not the Equal of Humans." 1 *Philosophical Exchange* (Summer 1974).

Martin, Alexander; Zim, Herbert S.; and Nelson, Arnold L. *American Wildlife and Plants: A Guide to Wildlife Food Habits*. New York, 1951.

Martin, Ernest W. *The Case Against Hunting*. London, 1959.

Martinengo-Cesaresco, Evelyn L.H. *The Place of Animals in Human Thought*. London, 1909.

Mason, Jim and Singer, Peter. *Animal Factories*. New York, 1980.

McManus, John. "An Economic Analysis of Indian Behavior in the North American Fur Trade." XXXII *Journal of Economic History* (March 1972): 36-53.

Meitzen, Manfred O. "The Ethics of Hunting: A Christian Perspective." 16 *Dialog* (Winter 1977): 57-61.

Midgley, Mary. *Beast and Man: The Roots of Human Nature*. Ithaca, N.Y.: Cornell University Press, 1978.

Moncrief, L.W. "An Analysis of Hunter Attitudes Toward the State of Michigan's Anterless Deer Hunting Policy." Ph.D. dissertation, Michigan State University, 1970.

Moore, Patrick (ed.). *Against Hunting*. London, 1965.

More, Thomas, "Motivational Attitudes of Licensed Massachusetts Hunters." M.S. thesis, University of Massachusetts, 1970.

Morris, Richard K. and Fox, Michael W. *On the Fifth Day: Animal Rights and Human Ethics*. Washington, D.C., 1978

Morse, Mel. *Ordeal of the Animals*. Englewood Cliffs, N.J , 1968

Narveson, Jan. "Animal Rights." 7 *Canadian Journal of Philosophy* (March 1977): 161-178.

National Geographic Society. *Wild Animals of North America*. Chicago, 1960.

National Wildlife Federation. "Endangered Species" (special issue). XII *National Wildlife Federation* 3 (Apr May 1974).

Ortega y Gasset, Jose. *Meditations on Hunting*. New York, 1972.

Osborn, Fairfield. *Our Plundered Planet*. Boston, 19/8

Parsons, John E. "Gunmakers for the American Fur Company." XX-XVI *New York Historical Society Quarterly* (1952): 181-193.

Pearson, Henry A. *Starvation in Antelopes with Stomachs full of Feed*. U.S.D.A. Forest Service Research Note No. RM-148.

Peterle, T.J. "Characteristics of Some Ohio Hunters." 31 *Journal of Wildlife Management* 2 (1967): 275-289.

_____. "The Hunter: Who is He?" 26 *Transactions* of the North American Wildlife and Natural Resources Conference (1961).

Phillips, John C. "Wild Birds Introduced or Transplanted in North America." 61 *U.S.D.A. Technical Bulletin* (1928).

Point, Nicholas. *Wilderness Kingdom*. New York. 1967.

Potter, Dale *et al. Human Behavior Aspects of Fish and Wildlife Conservation,* Technical Report of U.S. Forest Service, PN No. 4. 1973.

Randle, Allan C. "Relationship of Predatory Control and Big Game Problem Areas." *Transactions* of 8th North American Wildlife Conference (1943): 329-333.

Ray, J. Arthur. *Indians in the Fur Trade: Their Role as Trappers, Hunters and Middlemen in the Lands Southwest of Hudson Bay, 1660-1870*. Toronto University, 1974.

Regan, Tom. "An Examination and Defense of One Argument Concerning Animal Rights." 22 *Inquiry* (Spring-Summer 1979).

_____. (ed.). *Matters of Life and Death*. New York, 1979.

_____ and Singer, Peter (eds.). *Animal Rights and Human Obligations*. Englewood Cliffs, N.J., 1976.

Regenstein, Louis. *The Politics of Extinction*. New York, N.Y. 1975.

Reiger, John F. *American Sportsmen and the Origins of Conservation*. New York, 1975.

Riter, W.E. "Predator Control and Wildlife Management." *Transactions* of 6th North American Wildlife Conference (1941): 294-299.

Ryder, Richard and Paterson, David (eds.). *Animal Rights: A Symposium*. London, 1979.

Salt, Henry. Animals' Rights. London, 1892, 1980.

Scharf, John A. 'The urgent Matter of Hunting Values and the Quality Crisis." 31 *Conservation Volunteer* 181 (1968): 15-25.

Scheffer, Victor B. *A Voice for Wildlife*. New York, 1974.

Schweitzer, Albert. *The Animal World of Albert Schweitzer* (C.R. Joy, ed.). Boston, 1951.

Shaw, Dale L. and Golbert, D.L. "Attitudes of College Students Toward Hunting." *Transactions* of the 39th North American Wildlife and Natural Resources Conference (1974): 157-162.

Shaw, George Bernard. "Killing for Sport" in Hamalian, L. and Volpe, E.L. (eds.), *Great Essays by Nobel Prize Winners*. New York, 1960.

Sievers, Ruth "To Check the Action of Destructive Causes." *NRA Conservation Yearbook* (1975): 22-35.

Simak, Clifford D. *Tribolite, Dinosauer, and Man*. New York, 1966.

Singer, Peter. *Animal Liberation: A New Ethics for Our Treatment of Animals*. New York, 1975.

__ _____ "The Fable of the Fox and the Unliberated Animals." 88 *Ethics* (Jan. 1978)· 119-125.

Stich, Stephen P. "Do Animals Have Beliefs?" 57 *Australasian Journal of Philosophy* (March 1979): 15-28.

Stokes, Gerald L. "Outdoor Activity and Personality." M.S. thesis, University of Georgia, 1966.

Taylor, Walter (ed.). *The Deer of North America*. Harrisburg, 1956.

Teague, Richard D. (ed.). *A Manual of Wildlife Conservation.* Washington, D.C., 1971.

Trefethen, James B. *An American Crusade for Wildlife.* New York, 1975.

Trigger, Bruce G. "The Jesuits and the Fur Trade." 12 *Ethnohistory* (Winter 1965): 30-53.

Trippensee, Reuben Edwin. *Wildlife Management,* Vols I & II. New York, 1953.

Tucker, Pat T. "Buffalo in the Judith Basin" in Merriam, H.G. (ed.), *Way Out West.* University of Oklahoma, 1969.

Turner, Ernest S. *All Heaven in a Rage.* London, 1964.

Udall, Stewart L. *The Quiet Crisis.* New York, 1963.

United States Forest Service. *Wildlife Habitat Improvement Handbook.* Washington, D.C., 1969.

Vogt, William. *Road to Survival.* New York, 1948.

Waterman, Charles F. *Hunting in America.* New York, 1973.

Webb, Walter Prescott. *The Great Plains.* New York, 1931.

Webb, William L. "Public Use of Forest Wildlife: Quantity and Quality Considerations." 66 *Journal of Forestry* 2: 106-110.

Wodziki, K.A. "Introduced Mammals of New Zealand." 98 *Research Bulletin* of the New Zealand Department of Science and Industry (1950).